MISSISSIPPI MOONSHINE POLITICS

MISSISSIPPI MOONSHINE POLITICS

How Bootleggers & the Law Kept a Dry State Soaked

JANICE BRANCH TRACY

THE
History
PRESS

Published by The History Press
Charleston, SC 29403
www.historypress.net

Copyright © 2015 by Janice Branch Tracy
All rights reserved

First published 2015

Manufactured in the United States

ISBN 978.1.62619.760.2

Library of Congress Control Number: 2014957213

This book is dedicated in memory of Hazel Brannon Smith and William Hodding Carter II, both well-known Mississippi journalists who used the power of the press in the best way of all—ensuring the people's right to know. Without their efforts in reporting the news, much of this story would not have been possible.

There is a tide in the affairs of men, which, taken at the flood, leads on to fortune.
—*William Shakespeare*

Contents

Contents

Preface

G rowing up in a state where the sale of alcohol was illegal did not seem unusual to me or to others around me. And other individuals who lived in Mississippi during its years of state prohibition will remember how simple it was to buy moonshine or bonded liquor. When a man, woman or, in many instances, young minor wanted to buy alcohol of any type or size, they could do so, provided they had the cash, knew where to go and were not afraid they would be arrested. Although liquor was sold illegally throughout the state, its sales were more concentrated in several regions, specifically the Mississippi River towns, counties in the Delta, Rankin County east of Jackson and the three-county area that encompassed Biloxi and Gulfport, located along Mississippi's Gulf Coast.

Prior to 1966, several small towns throughout the state became well known for their enclaves of liquor dealers, juke joints and nightclubs. One of these places was Durant, a Holmes County railroad town located on U.S. Highway 51 about an hour or so north of Jackson where numerous liquor and gambling establishments existed in the 1940s and 1950s. Across the Pearl River from Jackson, near the historic town of Brandon and the present-day Rankin County cities of Flowood and Pearl, the Gold Coast became a haven for local and out-of-state operators whose businesses offered illegal liquor and various other forms of entertainment. Throughout the Mississippi River counties, from Natchez along U.S. Highway 61 north to Clarksdale and beyond, illegal liquor was as plentiful and as available as water from the Big Muddy. Between the 1940s and early 1960s, the historic river town of

Vicksburg became a haven for several large illegal liquor wholesalers who purchased their supplies from Louisiana, just across the river, where alcohol was not only plentiful but also legal. And numerous other rural counties north, east and south of Jackson were well known for their moonshine and illegal bonded liquor operations.

The best-known area of all illegal liquor activity statewide, however, may have been Mississippi's popular resort destination referred to as the "Mississippi Gulf Coast." Elegant hotels, restaurants and rowdy nightclubs alike sold liquor openly along the thirty-five-mile stretch of sandy Gulf of Mexico beaches, long before the present-day chain hotels and Las Vegas–style casinos were built. Among the better-known Gulf Coast resort hotels and nightclubs that sold illegal liquor to guests were the Isle of Caprice Hotel and Resort, the Markham Hotel, Broadwater Beach, the Edgewater Gulf, the Buena Vista Hotel and Resort, the White House and the popular Gus Stevens Lounge. In 1951, the Kefauver Hearings brought nationwide attention to the Mississippi Gulf Coast area, focusing particularly on illegal gambling and liquor and their effects on airmen stationed at Biloxi's Keesler Air Force Base. Between 1952 and 1962, three state governors ordered National Guard raids on Gulf Coast liquor and gambling establishments.

In early 1966, a February raid on the Jackson Country Club in north Jackson, Mississippi, brought state and national attention to the "liquor issue," a subject that Mississippi's residents and lawmakers alike had wrestled with for years. With the eyes of the country on the last holdout state in the nation, and a need for political change at its zenith, Mississippi lawmakers decided to take action. A few months later, proponents of prohibition, as well as its increasing number of critics, witnessed a massive fusion of moral and legal suasion when the Mississippi state legislature passed a local option law. And when Governor Johnson signed the law that became effective on July 1, 1966, a new era of social change began in the state of Mississippi.

Acknowledgements

First, I want to thank my family for their patience and understanding during the extended period of time it took to write this book. They never complained when I suggested on numerous occasions that we go out to dinner after an all-day marathon of research, writing, editing and rewriting, especially when my mind and my body needed a serious rest. I especially appreciate my husband's willingness to listen as I read sections of the book aloud to him in an effort to test the clarity of the words I had written on someone else's ears. Secondly, I want to convey a world of gratitude to Christen Thompson, senior commissioning editor at The History Press, and to the rest of the publisher's staff, as well. Christen's knowledge and experience were invaluable to me, and her delightful personality and insightfulness made the entire publishing process a pleasant and enjoyable one. To Luster Bayless, Fred Blackwell, Jim H. Branch, Kathy Dodgen, Don Drane, Ken Hydrick Flessas, Tom Givens, Rusty Hanna, Barbara Jones Kincaid, Darryl Lewis, Davie Ricardo Lindsey, Bill F. Minor, Ross Nesbit, Allen Peacock, Gene Harlan Powell, Keith Roberts, Cheryl Taylor, Anne Vanderveert, Pete Walker and numerous other unnamed individuals who contributed official information, personal details and photos and who shared true stories with me about Mississippi's "liquor issue," I can't thank you enough. Your personal memories, experiences and extensive knowledge of life, liquor and politics in mid-century Mississippi contributed both realism and understanding to an often misunderstood subject, time and place.

Introduction

At least one author, Clay Risen, has written that our nation "was a drinking culture from the start." In an article entitled "How America Learned to Love Whiskey," published in the December 6, 2013 edition of *National Journal Magazine*, Risen described the ship that brought Puritans to America. "The *Arabella*…transported 10,000 gallons of beer, 120 casks of malt, and 12 gallons of gin. Alcohol was a necessity to the first settlers, not just for pleasure but also for health: Water was notoriously unhygienic." Risen wrote that by 1770, the 2.1 million American colonists had "consumed some 8 million gallons of rum" and that "between 1800 and 1830, annual per capita consumption of liquor, primarily whiskey, hovered around 5 gallons, the highest in American history."

Mississippi's issues with liquor officially began in Adams County in 1799, when the first territorial legislative body convened in the town of Natchez. An account of the first legislative session of the Mississippi Territory, over a decade before statehood, appeared in Reverend Thomas Jefferson Bailey's *History of Prohibition*, a book that was published in 1917 by Hederman Bros., former publishers of Jackson's current newspaper, the *Clarion-Ledger*. Other historical documents show that laws relating to "intoxicants" were passed during that same session. A provision in the laws outlined the process for issuing permits to sell intoxicants, specified quantities that could be sold and mandated amounts of fines to be levied for violations.

The movement to outlaw liquor, however, did not begin in Mississippi or even in the nation's capital. Efforts to stop the drinking of alcohol, later called the temperance movement, began in New England in the 1840s. At its inception, the movement's efforts were intended to eliminate the ill effects of alcohol on society, in general, by simply stopping the consumption of the liquor. But in 1851, Maine took that goal a few steps further when it became the first state to forbid the substance's manufacture and sale. Although the temperance movement lost some of its strength during the Civil War, it regained momentum afterward through the efforts of a recently formed Prohibition Party and the Woman's Christian Temperance Union. Members of these two groups and their affiliates reveled in their successful push against alcohol when Kansas voters passed an amendment to the state's constitution in November 1880 that banned the consumption of alcohol. The groups' successful crusade and the subsequent vote focused national attention on Kansas as the first state to pass such an amendment, and the next year, in May 1881, Kansas legislators added another law to the state's books, making the manufacture of alcohol illegal, as well. Once Kansas had taken a strong legal stance against alcohol, a number of other southern states, including Mississippi, eventually followed the lead of the Prairie State's lawmakers and voters.

A common thread existed among voters and lawmakers in southern states that passed later prohibition laws; both groups shared conservative political views and strong religious beliefs that alcohol was abhorrent to society. Mississippi's issues with alcohol, including its physical effects and the social problems frequently surrounding the substance, were not unlike those in other states. But unlike some of the midwestern and northern states, where non-Protestant religions often were unopposed to the manufacture, sale and use of alcohol, Mississippi's conservative religious society fiercely fought for laws that so many believed would end, or at least control, the socioeconomic problems created by alcohol. Allegedly, the state's anti-alcohol groups held their first prohibition meeting in Mississippi in 1881, but it was not until 1886 that state legislators passed a local option law allowing state residents to vote in local elections to determine if their locale would allow or ban the sale of alcohol.

Enforcement of liquor laws in Mississippi was never easy, however, and it became even more difficult in the years that followed. A transcript of the House Ways and Means Sub-Committee No. 3 on Internal Revenue meetings held on February 3 and 5, 1906, stated that Mississippi congressman B.G. Humphreys addressed a bill he had introduced, H.R. 4533, intended "to amend the internal-revenue laws so as to provide for publicity of its records." Representative Humphreys argued that passage of the bill would assist his home state in enforcing liquor laws in place during that time period by requiring the internal-revenue collector "to give a certified copy of the tax receipt [to the state] which he issues to liquor dealers upon request." At the time Humphreys introduced his bill, the internal revenue collector's only requirement to disclose the identity of individuals who had purchased a federal special-tax license was a list of names he posted on his office wall.

During these committee meetings, Humphreys expressed his belief that numerous individuals who bought the federal licenses subsequently operated illegal businesses in various states, including Mississippi. He further provided statistics stating that "in the State of Mississippi, there are 123 licensed saloons and 557 'blind tigers.'" Henry De Lamar Clayton, who represented Alabama's 3rd District, and several other committee members, as well, agreed with Congressman Humphreys's concern that special-tax licenses issued to "blind tigers" operating in defiance of state liquor laws made it difficult for state law enforcement to prove a federal license had been issued. In his book, *Origins of the New South, 1877–1913*, Comer Vann Woodward explained some of the early prohibition laws passed in the South:

> *Until 1907, no state-wide prohibition law existed in the South; only three survived in the country, and none had been passed since 1889. Then in August 1907, Georgia passed a drastic state-wide law that touched off the third national prohibition wave, the first since the eighties. In rapid succession within the next nine months Oklahoma, Alabama, Mississippi, and North Carolina followed Georgia's example and Tennessee joined them in January 1909. Four of the six states acted through their legislatures, two by popular vote.*

When Mississippi's legislators first attempted to pass a state prohibition law in 1904, the majority vote (63–40) failed to meet the two-thirds required to enact the law. But persistence paid off, and in 1908, during the term of former governor Edmund Noel, state lawmakers enacted a statewide prohibition law that became effective on January 1, 1909. Citizen concerns about drinking and selling alcohol in Mississippi and elsewhere in the nation continued, however, and these concerns varied according to the individuals or groups who spoke out publicly against the substance. Economists and sociologists perceived alcohol consumption and its subsequent ills as economic problems; law enforcement saw the situation as a criminal problem; and Protestant churches and other religious groups agreed alcohol in general was a moral problem. But in post-Depression rural Mississippi, many folks simply saw making and selling moonshine and bonded liquor as alternate ways to earn a living during troubled economic times. A description of Mississippi's stance on the sale and shipment of liquor was included in the *New International Yearbook: A Compendium of the World's Progress*, published in 1914. Mississippi was described as "one of the most radical of the States in regulating liquor traffic." Collectively, the legislatures from 1912 to 1914 prohibited sale and import of liquor as well as gave the governor the power "to remove derelict officials." By 1913, cities with populations of five thousand or more—including Jackson, Vicksburg, Natchez, Meridian and Hattiesburg—were all under no-license.

Although Mississippi's state prohibition law outlawed the manufacturing, sale and traffic of liquor in the state, manufacturing, shipment and the sale and consumption of liquor were still allowed throughout most of the United States. But when the Eighteenth Amendment to the U.S. Constitution was passed on January 29, 1918, effectively banning the manufacture, sale and transportation of alcohol across the United States, Mississippi became the first state to ratify it. Language in the amendment allowed the states seven years to vote "yes," and individuals throughout the country were surprised when ratification by a three-fourths majority took only thirteen months, allowing the law to become effective on January 16, 1920. In a statement shortly after the amendment passed, Mississippi governor Theodore Bilbo reported that crime and incidental legal costs were down 80 percent and that the "civil, economic and moral life" of Mississippians was better than ever. Touting their early teetotaling, Bilbo predicted that Mississippi's residents "practically unanimously will vote to make the whole world dry." Similarly, the *Gulfport Daily Herald* lauded the prospect of national prohibition for Mississippi. In an editorial in March 1917, the paper pronounced that the liquor question only resulted in "hypocrisy and deception, law-breaking, agitation, bitterness and meanness" for Mississippi; they should be glad to be rid of it. Though the editorial stated that there was little local support in coastal communities, it denounced the prospect of bootlegging schooners under the opinion "that the gulf coast will be dry—at least dryer than it has been for a number of years."

On October 28, 1919, the Volstead Act, otherwise known as the National Prohibition Act, was passed. Language in the new law specifically granted the federal government enforcement power that had been omitted in the amendment. The Volstead Act also granted the states authority to enforce the ban on alcohol by passing what each state considered "appropriate legislation." Although Woodrow Wilson initially vetoed the act, Congress overrode his veto, and the law that granted enforcement of the ban on alcohol went into effect on January 16, 1920. As a result of the Volstead Act, Treasury Department agents became the federal government's first line of attack in the enforcement of the nation's new law regarding alcohol. Contrary to what many believe, *drinking* alcohol was never illegal during national Prohibition. And neither the Eighteenth Amendment nor the Volstead Act ever barred the consumption of alcohol but only regulated the manufacture, sale and transportation of liquor for mass consumption.

The move to end national Prohibition began on December 6, 1932, when Senator John Blaine of Wisconsin submitted a resolution to Congress that became the basis for the Twenty-first Amendment. On December 5, 1933, one day short of a year after the amendment was passed, Utah became the thirty-sixth state to ratify it, effectively making the amendment law and officially ending national Prohibition. Historical accounts of the events that followed the end of Prohibition show that tremendous numbers of the nation's residents celebrated. In fact, many individuals believed the day was one of the happiest they had experienced in the dark and tumultuous days since the Great Depression. During the next several months, Maine and Montana ratified the amendment, and North Carolina and South Carolina each declined to hold conventions to consider the matter. Eight states— Georgia, Kansas, Louisiana, Nebraska, North Dakota, South Dakota and Oklahoma—took no action to convene or to consider the amendment. Other states eventually ratified the amendment and passed their own state liquor laws, and by mid-century, Oklahoma and Mississippi were the last two holdout states in the nation. When Oklahoma finally repealed prohibition on April 7, 1959, Mississippi became the only remaining state in the nation where the sale of alcohol was illegal. With its own state prohibition law in place since 1909, Mississippi continued to operate as a "dry" state, although beer was legalized in 1934, the year after national Prohibition ended.

In 1944, in response to the mammoth moneymaking statewide industry that illegal liquor sales had become, Mississippi legislators passed the so-called black market tax, a law that legislators believed would generate millions of dollars of revenue, over time, for the state. The unpopular tax did bring in more revenue than anyone ever anticipated, but it was later abolished in 1962, although the change did not become effective until 1964. Along with the controversial tax on illegal liquor sales, one of the most pervasive and troublesome matters that existed throughout state prohibition was the issue of protection money, paid by liquor dealers and club owners to local law enforcement in exchange for special treatment regarding the state's liquor and gambling laws. Liquor issues frequently became election issues, and officials throughout the state, particularly county sheriffs whose responsibilities included enforcement of the county's liquor laws, frequently were elected by a constituency who voted for the candidate least likely to shut down illegal liquor operations. And as the years passed, many state residents and numerous other individuals who watched from the sidelines believed Mississippi might be the "wettest" dry state in the country.

After years of controversy that included numerous state-ordered enforcement actions by national guardsmen against illegal liquor and gambling, in late spring 1966, the Mississippi state legislature addressed the state's "liquor issue" when it passed a local option bill. On May 21, 1966, Governor Paul B. Johnson Jr. signed the bill, making it law. The provisions of the new local option law allowing citizens to hold referendum elections went into effect on July 1, 1966. The law required a petition signed by 20 percent of the county's eligible voters to hold an election to decide if a county wanted to sell liquor, or be classified as wet. No election was needed if the county chose to remain dry. As part of the local option law, the State of Mississippi established the Office of Alcoholic Beverage Control (ABC), an agency that functions within the Mississippi State Tax Commission and operates a state-owned and centrally located wholesale liquor distribution center. Also, the ABC's enforcement division was formed and entrusted with the responsibility for investigating and enforcing civil and criminal violations of Mississippi's liquor laws. Although it is interesting that bootleggers still exist in the twenty-first century, it's not surprising, given the history of moonshine and illegal liquor in the state. Individuals who still engage in the manufacture and sale of moonshine in Mississippi, however, should know that ABC's alcohol agents, tasked with the enforcement of Mississippi's liquor laws, take their jobs very seriously.

Chapter 1

Liquor, Religiosity and Dry Politics

Vote dry but remain wet. This seemed to be the battle cry of Mississippi voters each time local option came up in the years before 1966. Will Rogers, the popular twentieth-century humorist, is credited with stating his opinion regarding Mississippi's long-standing liquor issue when he said, "As long as Mississippians can stagger to the polls, they will vote dry." In *North Toward Home*, noted author and Yazoo City native Willie Morris called the state's dryness "merely academic; a gesture to the preachers and the churches," and recalled his father declaring that the only difference between Mississippi and its wet neighbor Tennessee was that in Tennessee "a man could not buy liquor on Sunday." In the fifty-eight intervening years between 1908, when Mississippi passed its own prohibition law, and the passage of a local option law in 1966, the degree of illegal liquor enforcement largely was left to the discretion of county authorities, specifically the county sheriff. For example, on the Gulf Coast and in the counties along the Mississippi River, all heavy tourist areas, alcohol was sold openly, but the county sheriffs and local police departments frequently looked the other way. Counties that elected anti-alcohol sheriffs likely were dry, and counties with more liquor-friendly sheriffs generally turned a blind eye to bootleggers and liquor dealers. More often than not, Protestant churches and bootleggers also drew imaginary lines in the sand during local election campaigns.

VIGILANTES FOR JUSTICE

For more than five decades, discussions about illegal liquor and the actions of those who consumed it continued to dominate religious conversations throughout Mississippi, just as they had since temperance groups formed in New England in the 1800s. Of interest here is that C.B. Galloway, former bishop of Mississippi's Methodist Conference and revered by his peers for his support of constitutional prohibition, wrote *Handbook of Prohibition* as guidance for fellow Mississippians who followed the teachings of the Methodist Episcopal Church South. Another minister, Reverend Thomas Jefferson Bailey, who embraced the Baptist faith, wrote in the introduction to his 1907 book, entitled *Prohibition in Mississippi*, published by Hederman Bros., that "no moral cause vigorously advocated by the Christian people of any land has ever failed." Reverend Bailey further defended that statement in this paragraph from his book:

> *It is a matter of devout gratitude to every prohibitionist that the ministry of Mississippi is practically a unit in defending the drink habit and the drink traffic. The ministers of the state are the logical leaders in morals and religion, and it is almost certain that when they universally and enthusiastically espouse the promotion of any religious or moral movement, it will succeed.*

Citizens throughout the nation organized and complained about the availability of illegal liquor in their communities and the crime it attracted. Among the earliest of these organizations in Mississippi was the Woman's Christian Temperance Union (WCTU). South of Jackson, in Forrest County, a citizens' group composed of preachers, bankers, merchants and members of the local WCTU formed to fight bootleggers in the county. The group's initial meeting was reported in a newspaper article published on March 20, 1929, in Biloxi's *Daily Herald*. The "mass meeting [had been] called by a group of vigilantes" and was scheduled for that evening in Hattiesburg. The "self-appointed law enforcement league" planned to "shame the public into playing the part of good citizens by serving on juries when called…and by sitting in the court room during liquor trials [to] offer moral support to the officers of the court and the prosecution." One member of the group, Reverend J.W. Thompson, pastor of Broad Street Methodist Church in Hattiesburg, spoke on behalf of the fifty individuals present and explained that their purpose was "to denounce 'certain little jack-leg lawyers who are keeping these bootleggers from the tolls of the law.'" One of

Reverend Thompson's chief complaints centered on some local defense attorneys who had attempted to impeach testimonies of two undercover agents during a recent trial by "directing scathing remarks against two Forrest County constables." Mrs. J. Monroe Smith, president of the WCTU, "pleaded with the twenty or more women present…to attend every session of court when rum cases were being tried. 'The bootleggers are organized, so we, too, must be organized to fight them.'" The news article further stated that "Harold C. Norsworthy, former sheriff of Forrest County, was named president of the vigilantes."

In later years, Bruce Yandle explained the background for his "Bootlegger and Baptist" theory of economics as it relates to southern prohibition. While working at the Federal Trade Commission in 1983, Yandle said the case of Sunday

The Woman's Christian Temperance Union (WCTU) monument outside the Lee County Courthouse. *Courtesy of William Gatlin.*

liquor sales helped him understand the politics surrounding federal regulation. In states that went dry on Sundays, one could find Baptists and bootleggers on the same side. "The good Baptists just wanted the Lord's Day to be relatively alcohol-free. And the bootleggers just loved the idea of having one day without competition from the legitimate sellers."

It was no secret that Mississippi's law enforcement community, primarily county sheriffs, often were directly or at least peripherally involved in moonshine making and in the distribution and sale of illegal bonded liquor. It seemed to be common knowledge that voting for the "right" candidate in some counties might determine whether the bootleggers and liquor dealers continued to make a living or spend time in the state or federal penitentiary. Allegedly, during the 1930s and 1940s, bumper stickers on bootleggers' cars frequently promoted the candidate who was friendly to the liquor dealers. At the same time, county residents, particularly those with conservative religious beliefs, supported the local law enforcement candidate who promised to put the bootleggers and other illegal liquor dealers out of business. One candidate for the office of Holmes County sheriff, Richard F. Byrd, a former Lexington scoutmaster, promised during his campaign that if he were elected, he would shut down the county's illegal liquor and gambling operations. But Byrd's constituents soon found out that his allegiance to Holmes County liquor dealers and nightclub owners was much stronger (and likely more lucrative) than his pledge to voters. County law enforcement officials in areas where liquor sales were heaviest, including Rankin County, Mississippi River counties and the Delta and the Gulf Coast region, often were elected by voters who benefited most from illegal liquor sales. In his biography of former Mississippi legislator, tax collector, treasurer and governor William F. Winter, Charles C. Bolton calls out the common contradictory role of an elected county official in the politics of illegal liquor. Bolton wrote that by 1957, "the putatively dry state" boasted almost one thousand federal wholesale and retail liquor dealers, dispersed through fifty-one of its eighty-two counties. In those places with the most free-flowing liquor, law enforcement typically "declined to enforce the prohibition measures," and when they did, it was by and large arbitrary.

Norman Ritter, a writer for *Life* magazine, wrote an article entitled "Tax for Lawbreakers Only," published in the magazine's May 11, 1962 edition. Although Ritter's article primarily addressed Mississippi's so-called black market tax, he included a few examples of Mississippi's problems enforcing the state's decades-old prohibition law. One particular case involved an ingenious liquor dealer who built a store, aptly named County Line Store, that straddled the county line between Washington County (Greenville) and Bolivar County (Rosedale, Cleveland). The store's location allowed the liquor dealer to move his inventory easily from shelves on the Washington County side of the store to shelves on the Bolivar County side, or vice versa, depending on which county's sheriff was cracking down on illegal liquor sales.

Chapter 2

Bootleggers, Alcohol Agents and Survival Economics

O verall, state prohibition never had a big effect on the manufacture and sale of illegal alcohol in Mississippi, especially when it came to the Mississippi River counties and the Delta. However, two major life-changing events, both affecting residents of these geographic locations, may have been the reasons behind this phenomenon. First, the Great Flood of 1927 took away lives, property and jobs, leaving giant scars on both the landscape and the economy. And even before a small recovery was made, the Great Depression followed, creating a financial crisis unlike anything the nation had ever experienced. If a family was poor before the flood, the same family was poorer in the 1930s. Simply put, the Depression drastically changed lives and left indelible marks on a wage earner's ability to make a living. Large numbers of residents lost their homes and their jobs, and families scrambled to search for their next meals. Many rural residents, especially those who had never worked anywhere except on a family farm and were suddenly forced to rethink how they might earn a living, chose making and selling moonshine as a quick and steady source of ready cash. In retrospect, some men and women who made and sold moonshine in the '30s and '40s must have believed that operating a still and selling bootleg liquor were simply matters of survival economics.

Mississippi's heavily wooded rural areas, often on privately owned land, became ideal places to hide and maintain moonshine stills. Access to the stills frequently involved traveling deep into the woods on unpaved roads, and federal alcohol agents, or revenuers, as they were called, had tough jobs searching for the illegal operations. Dealing with individual moonshiners, however, was even more difficult and always dangerous, since stills were prone to fires and explosions and moonshiners as well as federal alcohol agents were armed. One of the most feared and better remembered revenue agents in Mississippi during the '40s and '50s was a man named Sam Newman. A few individuals who knew the man said Newman was able to "sniff out" and destroy even the best-hidden stills. Allegedly, in later years, Newman developed quite a reputation as a tough enforcer. One older man from Simpson County who remembers Newman well said the alcohol agent was feared by moonshiners throughout the state. He added that Newman "busted up" many rural stills and helped send dozens of moonshiners to jail, especially after he began using a small airplane to locate stills in remote rural areas.

TILLMAN BRANCH

One man who discovered early in life that making moonshine could result in jail time was Edward Tillman Branch, a bootlegger known simply as "Tillman." Born and raised in Attala County, most of Tillman's business operations, including the nightclubs he operated, were located in Holmes County, where he lived as an adult. Archived records at Parchman Prison Farm indicate that Tillman was one of the state's earliest bootleggers to serve time at the remote Sunflower County prison farm. Incarcerated in 1927 for "manufacturing and selling illegal liquor," Tillman was sentenced to serve a two-year term at Parchman, but in December 1928, he was among a long list of Mississippi inmates who received early releases as part of former governor Theodore Bilbo's now infamous "Christmas Pardon." Serving time at Parchman, however, did not change Tillman's attitude about making and selling illegal liquor, nor did it motivate him to alter his path in life. After a brief attempt to work in his older brother's sand and gravel operation near Sidon, Mississippi, Tillman continued his moonshine operations in Attala and Holmes Counties.

By 1950, Tillman had served two prison sentences in the Atlanta Federal Prison for manufacturing alcohol, and after his second release, he served a short stint in the military. But Tillman's true love kept calling, and he soon returned to what he knew and liked best—making moonshine and operating two nightclubs near Durant. Although Tillman continued to manage his farm and crops by day, most of his earnings came from selling moonshine at his clubs. In the late 1950s, after his clubs in Durant were raided by the National Guard, Tillman built a large juke joint on land he owned just off Highway 51, south of Goodman. The new club, the Blue Flame II, was known by locals simply as Tillman's Place. Most of the club's patrons thought Tillman's Place had it all—food, music, entertainment and an endless supply of moonshine that some called the best in the country. There was no age requirement to get into Tillman's club, but as patrons soon discovered once they were inside, Tillman ruled the juke joint with an iron fist and a pistol. Everything changed at the Blue Flame, however, just after midnight on Easter Sunday morning, April 14, 1963, when an eighteen-year-old black man, Matthew Winter, shot and killed Tillman Branch. Winter pleaded guilty to shooting Tillman after a disagreement and an altercation that occurred late Saturday night. An account of Tillman Branch's life as a bootlegger and juke joint owner, as well as the events surrounding his death, is documented in *The Juke Joint King of the Mississippi Hills: The Raucous Reign of Tillman Branch*. Although Tillman was a legend, he was only one of many other bootleggers who kept a steady stream of moonshine flowing from stills carefully hidden deep in the hills and swamps of rural Mississippi.

In the early '50s, many individuals believed that bootlegging was fast becoming a big business in Mississippi and elsewhere in the nation. One individual, Hodding Carter, former editor and publisher of Greenville's *Delta Democrat-Times*, addressed the issue in an editorial he wrote entitled "The Bootlegger and Legalization":

> *Bootlegging in wet states…can be properly handled by reduced taxes and an adequate enforcement agency. Bootlegging in dry states can never be prevented. People are going to buy liquor, in spite of and because of the moralizing of their neighbors, and if the bootlegger is the only source, they will buy from him. No enforcement agency, existing or contemplated, is adequate enough to cope with this determination.*

Throughout the early 1900s and well into mid-century Mississippi, federal agents working for the Justice Department and later the Treasury Department investigated federal alcohol violations in the state. Occasionally, the agents worked with local law enforcement to locate and destroy moonshine operations. Although agents worked throughout the state, concentrated

Unidentified federal agents, U.S. Bureau of Prohibition. *Courtesy of the Library of Congress, Digital Archives.*

enforcement activities more frequently occurred along the state lines and in the Mississippi Gulf Coast area, where interstate commerce violations also were involved. An Associated Press article published on February 6, 1961, in *The Delta Democrat-Times* reported that the federal alcohol and tobacco

Unidentified alcohol agents seen during a typical liquor raid, circa 1930. *Courtesy of the Library of Congress, Digital Archives.*

division of the Internal Revenue Service listed Mississippi as "9th in the nation in the number of arrests for liquor violations." The article further reported that "raiders seized 57 stills, 534 gallons of whiskey, 16 vehicles, and 47,396 gallons of mash, and arrested 32 persons." These figures, however, represented only one month, December 1960, and did not include arrests by local law enforcement officers.

Chapter 3

Trouble in Paradise

Industrious, independent, and indomitable" were three words that appeared underneath the senior photo of Hazel Brannon in her Alabama high school yearbook. And three better words did not exist to describe the attractive, ambitious University of Alabama journalism graduate. In 1936, Brannon purchased the *Durant News*, the small Holmes County town's weekly newspaper, with $3,000 in borrowed money. As the new owner, publisher and editor of the only newspaper in Durant, the young newspaperwoman began her career writing about the everyday lives of the town's residents and publicizing local events. After she successfully increased sales and subscriptions to the *Durant News*, the female editor, an anomaly during that time and in that place, soon purchased Mississippi's second-oldest newspaper, the *Lexington Advertiser*, located in Lexington, the seat of government in Holmes County and where the publication was printed.

Although responsibilities of two weekly newspapers kept Brannon busy, the young editor was single and enjoyed traveling abroad and writing about cultures she visited and people she met on her travels. On one of these trips, an around-the-world cruise, Brannon met her husband-to-be, the ship's handsome purser, Walter "Smitty" Smith. After a whirlwind courtship, the two became engaged. Smith soon resigned from his job aboard ship, and several months later, Brannon and her dashing fiancé married in a lavish southern wedding at the Durant Hotel.

Brannon Smith felt that her own personal life was almost perfect, but she found it difficult to ignore the adverse effects that illegal alcohol had

Hotel Durant, circa 1935. *Courtesy of Mississippi Department of Archives and History.*

on Holmes County's families. In an effort to make a difference, Brannon soon decided to take a stand for what she believed was right and reported in the *Lexington Advertiser* that "trouble was brewing in paradise." As Brannon Smith's newspaper subscriptions increased, Holmes County's illegal liquor sales increased as well, and the editor continued to write articles about illegal liquor's impact on families and the criminal activities that followed. Because of her strong social consciousness and a desire to report the truth, Brannon Smith routinely criticized Holmes County sheriffs for ignoring the liquor problems and accused them of accepting money from owners in exchange for protection of their liquor and gambling establishments. Several longtime Holmes County residents, who prefer their names be omitted from this book, still remember that bootleggers, bonded liquor dealers and gambling den owners alike supported and voted for the county sheriff who would allow them to remain open—even if it meant turning over a share of their profits. When Brannon Smith openly challenged the sheriff to shut down Holmes County nightclubs and gambling dens, he continued to ignore the enforcement responsibilities of his office.

On November 21, 1955, an article about Hazel Brannon Smith published in *Time* magazine and entitled "The Press: The Last Word" discussed her editorial campaign against gambling and bootlegging in dry Holmes County. The article reported on Brannon Smith's efforts in 1946 that resulted in a Holmes County grand jury investigation and, subsequently, sixty-four indictments involving liquor violations and her critical editorials that targeted Sheriff Byrd. The article particularly focused on a 1954 incident at a country store in Tchula when the sheriff placed himself squarely in her crosshairs. Approaching a group of young black men outside the store, the sheriff reprimanded one of them, twenty-seven-year-old Henry Randle, for yelling loudly and obnoxiously, something the lawman referred to as "whooping." The young man denied the charge, but the sheriff cursed and struck him. Randle attempted to protect himself but ran off after the sheriff drew his firearm and told him to "Get going!" Despite Randle's attempt to flee, Byrd allegedly shot him in the thigh. Brannon Smith reported the story and reached out to the sheriff for comment, though he gave none. Her ensuing article ran on the front page of the *Lexington Advertiser* and was awarded by the Federation of Press Women. Winning the award, she said, "The laws in America are for everyone—rich and poor, strong and weak, white and black. The vast majority of Holmes County people are not rednecks who look with favor on the abuse of people because their skins are black. Byrd has violated every concept of justice, decency and right. He is not fit to occupy [his] office."

In turn, Byrd sued Smith for libel in the amount of $57,500, denying Smith's report entirely. As *Time* reported, in spite of the testimony of a white physician who had treated Randle's wound, the jury believed the sheriff and gave him a verdict for $10,000 against Hazel Smith. She appealed to the Mississippi Supreme Court, charging that the libel verdict against her was "punishment for daring to criticize a white man for abusing a Negro." The article stated, "The state's high court unanimously reversed the Holmes County Circuit Court. Ruled Justice Percy Lee: Editor Smith's story had been 'substantially true. The right to publish the truth, with good motives and for just ends, is inherent in the Constitution.' Commented Editor Smith: 'I don't regard this as a personal victory, but rather as a victory for the people's right to know.'"

Hazel Brannon Smith, the woman and the editor, sincerely believed in "the people's right to know." And her numerous experiences as a journalist in a state where illegal liquor, gambling and racial inequity frequently fueled human motives and politics caused her to fight back against those who challenged her belief system in ways she probably never imagined. Without a doubt, it seemed that Brannon Smith's refusal to join the White Citizens' Council in Holmes County and the council's formation of a competing newspaper, the *Holmes County Herald*, in an effort to put her out of business, soon became the undoing of the *Lexington Advertiser.* Although Brannon Smith fought valiantly to save the newspaper she had nurtured and loved, in the long run, her efforts were unsuccessful. In 1964, however, Hazel Brannon Smith was rewarded for her journalistic efforts when she received one of the most coveted awards of all, a Pulitzer Prize for editorial writing, the first of its kind ever awarded to a woman.

Chapter 4

Durant, Mississippi

The Town That Wouldn't Die

Durant, in Holmes County, just north of Goodman, Mississippi, once was the epicenter of illegal liquor and gambling activity in north central Mississippi. In the 1950s, *Reader's Digest* published an article about the town and its many illegal liquor and gambling establishments, referring to Durant as "a town too tough to die." In September 2013, I interviewed Sonny McCrory, a Durant business owner and a distant cousin of mine, who lived in the area his entire life. During the interview, McCrory identified almost two dozen nightclubs and juke joints that operated along U.S. Highway 51 and Mississippi Highway 12 between 1940 and the early 1960s and provided me with names, locations and some ownership information for establishments he remembered. Sadly, McCrory died barely two months after we talked. During our conversation, McCrory explained that Durant's many nightclubs developed primarily because large numbers of Illinois Central Railroad employees lived and worked in the town. Several current and former residents of Durant who lived there between 1930 and 1960 also provided details about nightclubs and liquor-related businesses in the town.

Nightclubs in Durant

Owned and operated by M.M. (Marshall) Powell (known locally as Blackjack), his brother H.D. Powell and allegedly a member of the Lane

I. C. R. R. Depot, Morning Train, Aberdeen Branch,
Durant, Miss.

Above: Illinois Central Railroad Depot, circa 1935, Durant. *Courtesy of Mississippi Department of Archives and History.*

Left: Former location of the White Pig nightspot, now a private residence near Durant. *Author's photo collection.*

family, Rainbow Garden was one of the larger and more upscale of the early clubs in Durant. Operating as a restaurant and a nightclub, it also offered music and dancing. Individuals who remember the establishment recall that the back rooms of the club contained blackjack tables and slot machines and were visible only to customers who were inside the rooms. A Durant resident who worked at the Durant Hotel during her teenage years remembered the White Pig, a nightspot she said was owned by a man named Troop Lucas. The business was a combination beer joint and pool hall that offered card games and dice in the back. The building in which the White Pig operated was sold to Sadie Seymour in 1967 and presently is a private residence occupied by another owner.

The Blue Flame Café (aka Tillman's Place or the Spot) located on Highway 12, near the Big Black River Bridge, was operated by Tillman Branch, a well-known local bootlegger. A copy of a newspaper article contained in the Mississippi Sovereignty Commission files indicated that a shooting occurred in Branch's café in 1953 when Johnny Holmes, a black man from Pickens, Mississippi, shot Branch and a black female cook named Clytee Parks. The news account also noted that the establishment "catered primarily to blacks." Other Durant nightclubs operating during that same period included Breazeale's Torch Club, McNair's Place, Hillside Café, Wagon Wheel, H.L. Malone's Place, Jack O'Diamonds, Mile-O-Way, 51 Grille, John McBride's Place, the Green Lantern, John Tye's Place, Club 51 and Chuck's.

Individuals who remember the establishments said that most sold food and drinks, including whiskey, gin and moonshine. Some of the places also offered music, dancing, blackjack games, slot machines, dice and, allegedly, prostitution. Durant's location on Highway 51, which connected Memphis and New Orleans and ran through the middle of town, made it a convenient entertainment venue for locals and travelers alike. A few older individuals, men and women, who grew up in the town and lived there during the years when liquor was illegal believe the nightclubs thrived because of the town's location and the customer base provided by the large presence of Illinois Central Railroad employees. Another rather unusual factor affected the number of clubs in the small town, according to two individuals who grew to adulthood in Durant. Organized crime syndicates in Memphis, New Orleans and along the Gulf Coast often sent members of their organizations who were in trouble with local law enforcement to Durant, "where it was easy to hide out while they were on the run."

By the late 1940s, Durant had more than two dozen nightclubs and juke joints, and the town's public and domestic crime rate increased as the number of nightclubs grew. Fights broke out late at night, and shootings and stabbings were common, both inside and outside the clubs. Automobile accidents, often caused by drunken drivers, as well as domestic disturbances fueled by liquor and gambling losses, occurred more frequently.

As large numbers of servicemen returned home from World War II, many local men went to work for the Illinois Central Railroad, where decent-paying jobs were available. But when a family's wage earner spent his money on liquor and gambling, those affected most were women and children. One woman in her sixties, who lived in Durant until she was a young adult, sadly recalled that she and her younger brother picked up and redeemed for cash glass bottles they found scattered along the streets and around Durant's nightclubs each Sunday morning. She explained that she and her brother gave their mother the refund money to replace a portion of their father's earnings that he "drank up" or "gambled away" most weekends at Durant's liquor clubs.

Hiding the Hooch

Ross Nesbit, a former Durant resident during the 1940s who became mayor of Satartia, Mississippi, several decades later, recalled memories of growing up in a town where liquor establishments outnumbered churches and businesses. Since liquor was illegal and was not stored "out in the open" in the places that sold it, Nesbit explained that liquor dealers routinely hid moonshine containers and bonded liquor bottles "outside the building" until the supply inside the club needed replenishing. Nesbit recalled the better-known hiding places, stating that crawl spaces underneath wooden buildings were among the most common spots. He explained that most wooden structures built during that era had crawl spaces, since they sat on wooden foundations supported by concrete blocks. Other hiding places, Nesbit added, were "hand-dug holes out behind the nightclubs," covered with dirt and grass to conceal the locations from those who walked near them.

One of the more clever methods used to hide liquor bottles, Nesbit continued, was to submerge them in washtubs or other large containers on the bottom of small spring-fed ponds or lakes near the nightclubs. Nesbit remembered well the day he went to a local swimming hole with some young friends, a spring-fed pool that just happened to be adjacent to Durant's popular nightclub the Rainbow Garden. Nesbit described how he and his friends were racing with one another, diving to the bottom of the swimming hole, attempting to see who could resurface in the shortest time. Suddenly, one of the young men in the group hit a large metal tub sitting on the bottom of the swimming hole. Although the young man was unhurt in the incident, he was very surprised to find dozens of unopened liquor bottles packed tightly inside the tub. Nesbit recalled how he and his friends, fueled by their youth and curiosity, quickly discovered the washtub was rigged with a carefully hidden pulley, barely visible in the dense vegetation bordering the swimming hole. Apparently, the pulley device was used to hoist the tub to the surface when more liquor was needed inside the club. Nesbit laughed as he recalled the incident, one that could have gotten him and his friends into some serious trouble with the owner of the club, a man about town named "Blackjack" Powell, who was known to carry a gun. Nesbit laughingly remarked that he still wonders whose job it was to retrieve the bottles from the bottom of the swimming hole.

Liquor Dealers, Sheriffs and the Citizens' Group

Holmes County's enforcement of illegal liquor sales, gambling and other crimes that seemed to go hand in hand with alcohol was the primary responsibility of the local sheriff. Between 1946 and early 1960, three men and one woman occupied the office of Holmes County sheriff: Walter J. Murtagh, Richard F. Byrd, Andrew P. Smith and Smith's wife, Hattie "Hab" Coleman Cade Smith. During Hab Smith's term, her husband, former sheriff Andrew Smith, served as her deputy. The Holmes County sheriff's jurisdiction included numerous hot spots of illegal liquor activity, but nightspots in Lexington, the county seat, and in the well-traveled town of Durant were the most popular in the county. Archived newspaper articles, many of them written by Hazel Brannon Smith, editor of the *Durant News* and later the *Lexington Advertiser*, state that Walter J. Murtagh, the owner of a Ford dealership in Pickens, Mississippi, defeated incumbent sheriff Walter L. Ellis on a campaign promise that he would clean up the illegal liquor businesses in Holmes County and ensure the area became a decent and safe place to live. In the years that followed Sheriff Murtagh's election, however, towns and communities throughout Holmes County, and the town of Durant in particular, became crime-ridden havens for illegal liquor dealers who often promoted other unlawful activities, including gambling and prostitution. By early 1947, most law-abiding citizens in Durant were fed up with the criminal activities that dominated life in their small town. Although dozens of citizens had complained directly to Sheriff Murtagh that illegal liquor sales were rampant in Durant, they saw few enforcement results, and more than one individual had publicly asked for the sheriff's resignation. Murtagh openly pledged to "dry up the county," and District Attorney Howard Dyer Jr. of Greenville and County Attorney Pat M. Barrett of Lexington pledged to help. But the concern of Durant's citizens grew, and many of the sheriff's constituents believed he had failed to uphold the sworn duties of his office.

Meanwhile, about fifteen miles west of Durant, in Lexington, bootleggers and others who sold illegal bonded liquor were making more money than they could spend. Frequently on weekends in Lexington, bootleggers and their cronies flaunted new suits and drove big, shiny cars around the town square. It was evident that selling illegal liquor was a moneymaking enterprise, but the fast cash was attached to high stakes for individuals willing to take the risks. Also at risk were the families of numerous club patrons waiting at home for loved ones who more often than not arrived home drunk and broke. Hazel Brannon Smith addressed these liquor-related problems in one of her editorials. She wrote that more and more people were getting into the bootlegging business, which came to be known as one of the most lucrative professions in the county. The bootleggers' "joints" were off the main highways, back in the woods, but they'd have a good road going in so you could get in and out. Slot machines and crap tables were added so that people who came by the honky-tonk would stay longer, drink more and gamble until they ran out of money. Grocery money was being spent on gambling, and some young couples were having a hard time feeding themselves and their babies. There were only two or three places in the county that really went in for it big and put in crap tables, including the Rainbow Garden, which was housed in a building that had been used for years as an enclosed skating rink. The Powell brothers, who owned it, fixed the place up like a nightclub, and they had a large space for dancing. They brought in big-name bands from Chicago, and in back they had a gambling room. Of course, all this was illegal.

Booze, Betting and Blood on the Streets

As a young teenager, Ross Nesbit delivered newspapers in Durant, and his route included various nightclubs and liquor establishments. On one occasion, he recalled entering a local club he described as a "liquor joint down on 51 highway across from Ellard's" to "drop off a newspaper." As Nesbit walked in the door, he saw a man sitting at the bar with a drink in his hand, betting with the bartender on the number of pennies in the bartender's closed fist. Nesbit recalled the pennies the bartender used were contained in an enormous whiskey bottle that appeared to be almost three feet tall sitting on the end of the bar. Nesbit said the man placed a $100 bill on the counter each time he attempted to guess the correct number, within ten pennies, inside the bartender's fist. Still a young teenager, Nesbit was fascinated by the sight of so many $100 bills, explaining that he had seen only one or two such bills in his entire life. After he watched the betting episode for a few minutes, Nesbit left to complete his paper route. At the time he left, Nesbit said the man at the bar already had lost over $1,000.

Although he did not know the gambler, Nesbit believes the man may have been one of the "mobsters" his dad mentioned who came to Durant from Chicago or New Orleans to "cool off." He volunteered that although townspeople knew many of the liquor dealers and proprietors of the clubs around town, the individuals usually "left the town's residents alone." Nesbit added that most of the wealthy liquor dealers and club owners primarily socialized with one another, since their employees frequently were family members. Otherwise, Nesbit said, liquor dealers and club owners "kept to themselves." Although Nesbit never witnessed a shooting, stabbing or other such violent act in Durant, he did hear adult discussions from time to time concerning serious crimes that occurred in town. He personally saw the results of a few "bad incidents" as he delivered newspapers on his bicycle, including several situations where a local doctor who made house calls "was working on people on their front porches, trying to keep them from bleeding to death after they had been stabbed."

On May 13, 1947, in response to the town's ongoing desire and need for law enforcement action, some of the local residents met at the Durant School and formed a citizens' group. A newspaper article published in *The Delta Democrat-Times* on May 23, 1947, reported the group complained about Holmes County's "rampant liquor traffic" and declared its common goal was "obtaining law enforcement in Holmes County, particularly in regard to gambling and liquor." During the group's first meeting, Marvin McClellan was elected chairman, but he served in that position for a very brief period of time. A local newspaper article reported that the group held a special meeting several nights later, and McClellan resigned, blaming his resignation on a visit by "a certain party" who "informed him" that "as a civil service employee he could not take the leadership in such an organization." Charles A. Knott succeeded McClellan as a temporary chairman. The Greenville newspaper reported its contact, *Lexington Advertiser* owner and editor Hazel Brannon Smith, was present at the meeting attended by several hundred people, including a few bootleggers. The news article reported, "The citizens' group appointed a committee to formulate procedure for obtaining a more stringent law enforcement." When the meeting adjourned, Brannon Smith said, "approximately 30 bootleggers tried to start a fight by making slurring remarks at some of the group's members as they left the school." As it turned out, the dedicated law enforcement action requested by the citizens' group formed in 1947 did not occur until four years later.

OPERATION BLACKJACK

After more than a decade of illegal liquor, gambling and crime in Durant and surrounding Holmes County, Mississippi, state government officials, religious leaders and citizens' groups appealed to the governor's office for assistance. By early 1951, twenty-one liquor and gambling establishments, primarily in the town of Durant, had been targeted by Governor Fielding Wright for a raid by the National Guard. Dubbed Operation Blackjack, the raid was planned in secret and scheduled for the night of March 31–April 1, 1951. On March 28, just days before the raid was to be carried out, *The Delta Democrat-Times* reported Governor Fielding Wright's warning in a front-page article: "Bootleggers, gamblers, gangsters, mobsters, and other plain hoodlums planning on migrating to Mississippi need to stay out. The entire resources of the state will be available to all sheriffs, judges, prosecuting attorneys and other law enforcement officials if such persons move into, or attempt to move into, their jurisdiction."

A syndicated news account of the Durant raid appeared in the April 2, 1951 edition of *The Delta Democrat-Times*, reporting that Governor Fielding Wright and Holmes County sheriff Ellis Wynn—the state's first sheriff to accept National and State Guard assistance to regulate bootlegging—deemed the raids a success. Wynn said they left the county "bone-dry and law-abiding." The twenty-one-roadhouse raid "yielded a prize of 25 persons under arrest, 'bushels' of corn liquor and whiskey confiscated, a dozen miscellaneous firearms in back, and a truck load of gambling equipment," as well as "evidence of liquor, gambling and firearms violations of law" in a third of those searched. Wynn said he "is confident the raids have rid his county" of this type of misdoings and that "this is the beginning of the end of racketeering in Holmes County. This raid has done a lot toward cleaning up the place. From here on out we're going to be throwing out the racketeers who are here and we're going to grab the outsiders as they come in. If we need the guard again I'm going to ask the governor for them."

Most newspaper and other historical accounts of the Holmes County incident named the National Guard as the military unit involved in the raid. But author Barry Stentiford, in his book *The American Home Guard: The State Militia in the Twentieth Century*, explained that uniformed men who participated in Operation Blackjack actually were members of the Mississippi State Guard. Stentiford also confirmed what newspapers covering the story had stated: the raid on Durant's nightclubs was the first active-duty assignment for the State Guard. The State Guard of the Korean War, he said, was supposed to be a contingency that would never be used. Thanks to the need to enforce laws surrounding gambling and liquor, the 1951 Mississippi State Guard activity in Holmes County provides one of the few recorded examples of the State Guard troops on active duty in the United States during the Korean War.

Several local newspapers, including the *Lexington Advertiser* and Jackson's evening newspaper, the *Jackson Daily News*, reported details of the Holmes County raid and included a hand-drawn map entitled "Map Used by Guardsmen in Operation 'Blackjack.'" The map marked the location of each of the twenty-one clubs targeted by the business name known to patrons and included the presumed name of each establishment's owner. Although the majority of the nightclubs were located in Durant, along U.S. Highway 51 or Highway 12, a few of the establishments raided were located near the towns of Lexington to the west, West to the north and Goodman and Pickens to the south. The *Lexington Advertiser* published details of the incident that occurred overnight on March 31–April 1 in the newspaper's April 5 edition and stated the raid was made by order of Governor Fielding L. Wright on the request of Holmes County sheriff Ellis Wynn and county attorney Pat M. Barrett. Top officials of the Mississippi National Guard participated in the raid that included almost one hundred national guardsmen, state guardsmen and local law enforcement officials.

W. Pat Wilson, adjutant general of the state of Mississippi, and Colonel T.B. Birdsong, provost marshal of the Mississippi National Guard, were in charge. Colonel Victor L. McDearman and L.E. Birdsong were also present during the raid. Local law enforcement officials assisting with the raid were Deputy Sheriffs George Bailey and W.H. Roach and Deputy/Jailor W.H. Byrd. The article also included names of individuals arrested during the raid on various liquor and gambling charges: R.C. Holder, Floyd Head, John McBride, Mrs. John McBride, L.C. McBride, A.L. McNair, Jimmy McNair, D.W. Broyles, H.D. Powell, M.M. Powell, Mrs. H.S. Powell, Dennis Williams, Mary M. Burnett, Marie B. Johns, J.G. Lane, Judson Lee Drane, John Pettus, Herbert Downer, Jessie Mae Waddell, Lillian B. Pate, John D. Pate, John D. Pate Jr. and H.L. Malone Jr. Individuals who assisted with post-raid administrative details at the Holmes County sheriff's office were Mrs. E.E. Wynn and Mrs. Clara Ginn Bruce, assistants to Sheriff Wynn. Possibly the largest cache of illegal liquor and gambling paraphernalia confiscated during the raid was discovered at Blackjack Powell's Rainbow Garden in Durant. According to the Lexington newspaper's account of the incident, "slot machines, counter pay type, punch boards, poker chips, dice, brass knucks, whiskey, cartridges, and shot gun shells" were confiscated from Powell's nightclub. Additional items were removed from "Mrs. H.S. Powell's residence north of Rainbow Garden," including "one Chevrolet pickup truck loaded with thirty-nine gallons of moonshine whiskey, and eight gallons of moonshine in [the] storm cellar of the house." The estimated value of contraband liquor and gambling equipment confiscated at the Rainbow Garden alone was approximately $25,000.

Greenville's newspaper, *The Delta Democrat-Times*, reported on April 19, 1951, that attorneys for John Pettus, one of the individuals on trial for illegal possession of liquor, asked Circuit Judge Arthur Jordan "to dismiss the case on the grounds that Gov. Fielding Wright sent the troops into Holmes County at Sheriff Ellis Wynn's request without proper authority under the state constitution…Since evidence against all 21 indicted was seized with the aid of the troopers, it is suspected that if Judge Jordan shall sustain the defense motion in the [John] Pettus case, the ruling would also throw out the evidence in all of the cases." Also present when circuit court opened that day were Stanny Sanders, district attorney; Miss Minnie Jordan, circuit clerk; and Miss Pearl McLellan, court stenographer. Interestingly, Pettus was among several dozen men and women who were arrested almost a decade later in another raid, one that some have referred to as the largest state and federal moonshine raid ever conducted on Mississippi soil.

Bill Minor Recalls the Raid

One of the non-military, non–law enforcement officers present during the raid on Durant was William F. "Bill" Minor, a well-respected journalist who currently lives in Jackson, Mississippi. Now in his early nineties, Minor is a native of Baton Rouge, Louisiana; a Tulane University graduate; and a military veteran. As the bureau chief of the *Times-Picayune* in Jackson, Minor recalled that he accompanied members of the National Guard and law enforcement as they implemented the overnight raid dubbed Operation Blackjack. During a telephone interview with Minor on July 2, 2014, the longtime journalist explained his involvement in the raid and provided recollections of what happened in Holmes County in early 1951.

Minor recalled that the process first began when Governor Fielding Wright signed an executive order for the enforcement action that called for the raid. Reports made to the governor's office that open sales of illegal liquor had been observed in a particular locale were the basis for the order. In this particular instance, citizens' complaints about Holmes County liquor and gambling establishments, particularly those in Durant, had triggered the governor's action. Once the order was signed by the governor, his staff sent a copy to the general in charge of the state military unit. Minor explained it was common practice for a member of the general's staff at the National Guard offices to notify a few news journalists that a raid was planned for a certain time and place. In the instance of the Holmes County raid, Minor said he was one of two newsmen notified. All planning for the raid was executed with the utmost secrecy, Minor recalled, and even the military men who were selected to participate in the raid were unaware of the exact location or the names of the designated targets. Minor remembered that he was told to meet up with the groups participating in the raid, and he and another news reporter drove to the designated meeting spot in a remote area of Holmes County, where the staging of the raid took place.

Although Minor did not remember the names of the clubs raided overnight on March 31–April 1, 1951, he did recall some of the actions that took place. Most of the guardsmen, he said, were armed with guns and axes. Minor explained the axes were used to destroy cases of illegal liquor and slot machines the guardsmen found in the back rooms of some of the clubs. Minor added that images of the mangled pieces of metal remaining after slot machines had been destroyed with an axe still remain one his most vivid memories of the Durant raid. He remarked that *Lexington Advertiser* publisher and editor Hazel Brannon Smith wasn't notified of the Durant raid, and he still remembers the moment she drove up beside him in her white Cadillac convertible and asked why he had received advance notice of the raid and, as the editor of the Lexington newspaper, she had not. Although Minor didn't elaborate on the conversation, he volunteered that he and Brannon Smith, as fellow journalists and members of the Mississippi Press Club, successfully forged a long friendship and a professional relationship in the years that followed, in spite of the incident beside her car that day in Durant.

DURANT RESIDENTS REMEMBER THE RAID

Barbara Jones Kincaid, who lived in Durant when she was a young child, vividly recalled the night of the raid on the Mile-O-Way nightclub located on Highway 51, just south of downtown Durant. Kincaid is the daughter of Dorothy Drewry and Cecil Jones, but at the time of the raid, she was living with her step-grandparents, R.C. Holder and Jessie Head Holder, who managed the establishment. Kincaid explained that she and her family occupied living quarters inside the building, in the back of the area dedicated to the club's activities. Sometime later, Kincaid said, her stepfather, Donald Broyles, ran the Mile-O-Way. During an interview with Kincaid in early 2014, she explained that she currently helps her brother manage Kaffay Mile-O-Way, a popular Durant restaurant currently operating inside a remodeled version of the building that once housed the Mile-O-Way Inn.

On the night of the raid, Kincaid recalled that she was awakened from a sound sleep by loud voices of men storming into the wooden building. Some of the men were in uniforms, she said, and they were armed with guns and axes. As Kincaid recalled the morning of April 1, 1951, her eyes reflected the fear she still remembered as she described events occurring inside the building that was her home as a four-year-old child. As Kincaid observed the armed men in uniforms from behind a child's mask of terror, she watched them use axes to "hack up" the wooden floor in the club and in her family's living quarters. Kincaid distinctly remembers hearing some of the men say they were looking for whiskey they believed was hidden underneath the building's wooden floor. Although the incident at the Mile-O-Way Inn occurred over fifty years ago, Kincaid recalled how afraid and distrustful she was of anyone who wore a uniform. This feeling, she says, continued to haunt her for many years after the raid.

Former location of the Mile-O-Way nightclub, now operating as Kaffay Mile-O-Way Restaurant. *Author's photo collection.*

Ross Nesbit also remembered the 1951 raid, now an infamous event in Durant's history. When asked about the origin of the raid's name, Nesbit explained the raid may have been named for Blackjack Powell, one of the two Powell brothers who owned the Rainbow Garden nightclub. Nesbit described Rainbow Garden as a large restaurant and dance hall, one of Durant's oldest and finest, and Blackjack Powell as a "man about town, a snappy dresser, who drove a very nice car." Although he was living out of state in 1951, Nesbit recalled reading a *Reader's Digest* article several years later entitled "The Town Too Tough to Die." The article, he explained, profiled Operation Blackjack in the story about Durant's era of illegal liquor and gambling clubs.

And as it happened, the town of Durant certainly did not "die" after the raid. In fact, liquor sales and gambling activities soon resumed, and life in Durant continued almost as it had before. Although some club owners closed their establishments, others moved to new locations away from Durant. But the restaurants and clubs that remained in town survived, in part, because they continued to sell liquor to customers who wanted it. The raid did have a lasting effect, however, on a few liquor and gambling establishments that changed their names, relocated or attempted to operate in a much more cautious manner. Some of the better-known Holmes County establishments that sold illegal liquor in the years that followed were the Blue Flame and Branch's Grocery, operated by Tillman Branch near Goodman; Grape's Camp, near Pickens; and Mandy's Place, named for Mandy McLean.

MCLEAN V. STATE OF MISSISSIPPI

After Andrew P. Smith was sworn in as sheriff of Holmes County in 1956, he attempted to make good on a campaign promise to curtail illegal liquor sales and other criminal activities in his county. One of the liquor establishments Smith targeted for enforcement during his initial year in office was Mandy's Place, located off Highway 12 near Durant. The exterior of the club, named for Mandy McLean and operated primarily by Ed McLean, appeared to be that of an old service station, but the interior of the popular hangout contained a counter, tables and a jukebox. Neither food nor music, however, was the main attraction at Mandy's Place—it was the bar and the illegal liquor that made customers return.

The text of a Mississippi Supreme Court decision in the case of *McLean v. State 230 Miss. 894* (1957) *94 So.2d 231* stated that Sheriff Smith, on September 13, 1956, enlisted the assistance of two Yazoo County deputies, W.T. Stubblefield and W.B. Chapman, to "aid in apprehending violators of the liquor law." Specifically, Smith gave the deputies ten dollars in cash and instructed them to purchase liquor at Mandy's Place near the Holmes/Attala County line. After Stubblefield and Chapman had picked up the cash at Sheriff Smith's office in Lexington, they traveled to Mandy's Place, where they "took a seat at the counter and ordered two cans of Falstaff beer." The high court's decision continued, stating that the appellant, Ed McLean, was "behind the counter and waited on them." The deputies said the two of them drank the beer, and each man ordered another. After McLean took their order for a second round of beer, Stubblefield asked "the appellant if he had any whiskey and he said he didn't have anything but V.O. and that it was $3.00 a pint. The appellant then left the presence of Stubblefield and Chapman remained away from five to twenty minutes and returned with a pint of whiskey. The appellant reached under the counter and got a sack and put the whiskey in it and delivered it to Stubblefield and Stubblefield paid for it."

Although Stubblefield and Chapman identified McLean as the individual who delivered the whiskey and who received the money in payment for the liquor, McLean vehemently denied the charge, stating he was outside listening to a ballgame during the time the deputies were inside and that he entered the premises only once or twice to get drinks of water. Additionally, McLean produced several witnesses who testified they saw Stubblefield and Chapman order beer at the counter, but the witnesses denied seeing either man leave with bottles of liquor. McLean's witnesses further testified that Doc Weems, and not Ed McLean, was tending the bar during the time that Stubblefield and Chapman were seated at the counter. On April 15, 1957, the decision handed down by the Mississippi Supreme Court affirmed McLean's initial conviction of "unlawful possession of intoxicating liquor," rendered earlier in justice of the peace court, District 3, of Holmes County.

Chapter 5

"Hell-Hole of the Delta"

Built along what many locals and visitors to Mississippi refer to as the "Blues Highway," or U.S. Highway 61, Leland, Mississippi, is one of the oldest towns in the Delta. Once home to several large plantations, this particular portion of Washington County is not only steeped in history and southern culture, but it also contains some of the richest farmland in the state. Historic Deer Creek runs through the town of Leland, and some of the oldest and finest homes, built by the town's earliest residents, line the scenic creek's meandering banks. During the years of state prohibition, however, there was another side to this part of Washington County, illustrated by Will Irwin in his 1908 *Collier's* article, "American Saloon." Irwin called Leland the "Hell-hole of the Delta." On Leland's two main streets, Irwin wrote, "every third or fourth business place is a saloon. On Saturday afternoon, the [farm] hands begin to come into town. From that time until Monday morning life in Leland is one black debauch."

To its credit, by the late 1940s, Leland had survived the vast devastation and loss of lives and jobs caused by the Great Flood of 1927, the bottomed-out economy of the Great Depression and the war years, when numerous men and women who left to serve their country on foreign battlefields never returned home. But four decades after Irwin's article was published, Leland's problems with liquor and gambling still existed, and many of the town's residents and civic leaders wondered if their hometown would ever overcome the name it had been given in 1908. A significant number of these individuals who believed that crime in Leland was totally out of control were concerned that illegal liquor was the root cause of the crime problem. On November 6, 1948, an unusually large number of local residents showed up at a city council meeting and voiced their concerns about the liquor issue. In an open letter published in the town's newspaper, the *Leland Progress*, resident Catherine Weston expressed her belief that citizens present at the council meeting wanted change:

> *Leland has become the bootleg center of the Delta and it certainly seems that citizens would want to help free the community from influences that weaken and degrade the lives of all the people. Since 1946, the number of liquor dealers has grown from 6 to 69 in Washington County. Of this number, 18 are in Leland and 7 are around Leland. Children need to see parents and adults take a firm stand against the situation as it is in Leland today.*

Leland's Garden Club also wrote to the newspaper, using the newfound contradiction of the town motto, "Leland—The City Peaceful, Prosperous, and Progressive," as its soapbox. "If Leland expects to live up to her motto, it is PAST time for us to do something about this gambling, dope selling, and bootlegging," the club wrote. Gently calling out its own beautification efforts, the club praised Leland's worth but lamented that its "young people are unfairly subjected to these temptations" and that they can't count on change until Leland "is CLEANED UP."

Two years later, in November 1951, the *Leland Progress* reported that a committee was being formed in Leland called the Good Citizens Committee. The committee was gathering signatures for a petition that stated that Leland's liquor law enforcement had for too long been lax, and the town had gained "an unfavorable reputation as a wide open town, and that such reputation seems likely to bring an influx of lawbreakers, such as dope dispensers and gamblers." The next month, December 1951, a newcomer to town expressed the opinion that town officials should address the concerns of five hundred citizens of Leland who had signed a petition asking for stronger enforcement against illegal liquor sales. The newcomer was among the citizens who signed the petition. The newcomer's plan was a citizen-action committee of sorts. From the five hundred who signed the original petition, officials would choose a group to confront bootleggers directly:

> *Let an officer say to such dealer… "From now on we are going to prosecute you if you continue to sell…Of course we know you must make a living,*

but anyone that has sense enough to make money selling liquor against the law has sense enough to make a good living within the law. However, if you go on selling as you have been, we will do all in our power to put you out of business."

Former Mayor Bill Caraway

In *I Was There: An Autobiography*, published in 1996 and written by former Leland mayor and state senator William Julius Caraway, known simply as Bill, the author describes what it was like to serve as mayor in a town once described as the "Hell-hole of the Delta." Born in Brookhaven, Mississippi, Caraway served in the United States Air Force during World War II before he began a teaching career in Mississippi. Caraway recalled in his autobiography that he had just accepted a teaching position near Leland when a Leland friend asked if he was interested in running for town mayor. Caraway explained that he had no experience in politics, but reluctantly, he agreed to run for the position anyway. In his autobiography, Caraway admitted that he did not take the election seriously and only campaigned the night before the election when he heard that local gamblers had given him 2:1 odds of winning. Caraway did win the election, but the margin of victory was a mere fifty-seven votes. Senator Caraway explained his new position paid $300 per month, or "about the same as a teacher made at that time." Caraway chronicled his years as Leland's mayor, stating that Washington County was wet, and on Saturday nights, "thousands of blacks" came to town, where they drank and gambled until late into the night. Since the chief of police also was an elected position, Caraway, as the town's mayor, had no authority over the chief or the department's officers. Although the former mayor's book contained no details of specific disagreements with the police chief or members of the police department, the simple fact that he and the chief maintained parallel offices must have created at least a few disagreements about the enforcement of illegal liquor and gambling in the town.

When Caraway was sworn in as mayor of Leland, he said the town had approximately 2,800 residents, seven liquor and gambling joints and one medical clinic with seven beds. The clinic was operated by the doctor who had established it, Dr. Bunk Witte. Caraway wrote that Dr. Witte was a kind and benevolent man who often remained at the small medical facility until the wee hours of the morning, particularly on the weekends, when he often stitched up people who had been stabbed or beaten during violent incidents at the town's nightclubs and juke joints.

Caraway recalled that one of his official duties as mayor included serving as Leland's municipal judge, explaining that Mississippi state law required all mayors of towns with populations of fewer than ten thousand people to serve collaterally as the town's judge. Serving on the bench of Leland's municipal court, Caraway recalled, was among his more memorable experiences during the time he served as mayor. As municipal judge, Caraway held court three days a week, on Monday, Wednesday and Friday, and his usual weekly caseload consisted of about one hundred cases, often involving individuals who were repeat offenders of liquor and gambling laws. One particular individual was the female owner of a gambling club, and Caraway said that she had an unusual habit of removing her coat and turning around a few times before she approached his bench. Apparently, word got back to Caraway through his cook that this particular woman had been heard around town bragging that she wanted the young judge to get a good look at her figure when she appeared in his court. The mayor became outraged at what he had been told and immediately vowed to shut down all seven gambling joints in Leland, including the club owned by the woman. And he kept his promise.

As a result of his action, Caraway soon faced an unexpected and larger civic issue, one more serious than any he had experienced as mayor. One local man who owned five of the seven liquor and gambling clubs shut down by Caraway was so enraged about the club closures that he initiated a chain of events that Caraway never forgot. In his autobiography, the former mayor detailed the events that followed. It all began when the angry owner of the five clubs dispatched one of his black male employees to downtown Leland, where he had been directed to visit a merchant who sold Florsheim shoes. Inside the store, the black man complained to the merchant, telling him the mayor had closed his boss's clubs in Leland. He also informed the merchant that his boss planned to "move his gambling houses over to Arcola" and warned the store owner that he and his friends would be taking their shoe business to Arcola in the very near future. The story of the man's visit to the store quickly spread like wildfire to other downtown merchants. The former mayor chronicled the incident in his autobiography, stating that "thirty-five local merchants showed up" at his office later that day, where they angrily berated him for closing the clubs and begged him to reopen the liquor and gambling joints. When Caraway told the group of merchants

Main Street, Leland, 1940s. *Courtesy of Mary Boteler on behalf of Ruth Stovall, deceased.*

that "under no circumstances" would he reopen the clubs, the group became more upset, and one of the merchants told the mayor that if he "caught him outside the city limits," he planned to "beat him up." The merchants eventually retreated, Caraway said, without further incident, and the man who promised bodily harm never acted on his threat.

The Hospital That Liquor Fines Helped Build

Eventually, Caraway allowed two of the seven liquor joints to reopen, with the understanding that they would move their operations outside Leland's city limits. Caraway wrote that he planned his next actions very carefully, with a purpose in mind. He explained that once the two establishments moved outside Leland's city limits, he visited them periodically. The two establishments openly sold illegal liquor, and on each of Caraway's visits, he purchased a pint of liquor from the proprietors. Since the dealer broke the law each time he sold liquor to Caraway, the mayor immediately charged the individual with selling illegal liquor. But instead of arresting the individuals, Caraway allowed the offenders to post a $100 bond for each violation. Subsequently, Caraway deposited the money in what he called a "hospital fund" that was used to cover treatment of charity patients at Dr. Witte's small medical clinic in town. Although Mayor Caraway's method of dealing with Leland's illegal liquor trade may have been somewhat unorthodox, the money he collected provided a much-needed benefit to Leland residents who could not afford medical care. The hospital fund continued to grow, and within a few years, the money was used to help build a new hospital in the small Delta town that so desperately needed a larger facility. Additionally, the state contributed $20,000 toward the new building, and the town issued $100,000 in bonds.

In 1954, the *Leland Progress* published a photograph of the almost complete, new and very modern hospital building. The one-story brick building, with a unique multicolored glass feature over the front door, included seventeen patient rooms, with a total capacity of thirty-two patients, and some private bathrooms. Less than a decade after the state's local option law was passed and money from the town's illegal liquor fines dried up, W.S. Witte Hospital, as the Leland health facility was known, ran into financial difficulty. On July 12, 1972, an article in *The Delta Democrat-Times* reported that Leland mayor T.K. Scott had requested $40,000 from the Washington County Board of Supervisors to help with the hospital's financial problems. The newspaper account also referenced Mayor Scott's statement from January of that year, saying, "The hospital once received revenues from the city's 'legal illegal liquor' [and recently had been receiving] about $1,000 per month in city funds and services."

Bill Caraway served thirteen years as mayor of Leland. When State Senator George Walker's term was about to expire in 1959, he suggested to Caraway that he should run for the vacant senate seat. Caraway acted on his

Leland Hospital under construction, circa late 1940s. *Courtesy of Daryl Lewis, historian.*

friend's suggestion and ran unopposed in the election. Subsequently, Senator Bill Caraway served twelve years in the state senate and was unopposed each time he ran for reelection.

Life and Liquor in Leland

A longtime resident of Leland remembered the days when liquor was sold openly in the town. For personal reasons, the man asked that his name be omitted from any reference in this book. He described one of the best-known liquor businesses in Leland as a drive-through store known to locals as Tin Top. The store got the name from its corrugated tin roof, and the man recalled the structure was "built like a barn." He knew the place well and described the store's walls as "overhead doors" that "rolled up and down." The doors, he said, remained up during operating hours, allowing cars to drive through and customers to make purchases without leaving their cars. The owner of the Tin Top, he said, was a man whose last name was Tabor, but another individual named Colon managed the establishment on a daily basis. The man recalled that Colon was the father-in-law of Louis Munn, a former mayor of Leland who was in office in 1966 when the state passed the local option law. The longtime Leland resident said that Colon owned a mixed-breed dog resembling the present-day pit bull breed, and he kept the dog at the liquor business. When Colon left a couple of times a day to go to town for coffee, he chained the dog and left him to guard the liquor store from would-be thieves. The man said the Tin Top's merchandise was never disturbed while the dog secured the premises.

The man stated that local liquor dealers bought their inventories from "the Fratesi brothers, Larry and Sam, who operated a store just outside of town." He further explained that Fratesi family members were longtime Leland residents and merchants and once operated a store that contained the largest liquor supply in Leland. Although he was uncertain about the source of their supply, the man suggested the Fratesi brothers may have purchased their liquor inventory from Louisiana dealers and transported the merchandise up the Mississippi River for offloading in swampy, secluded areas nearby.

When I asked the man if he recalled other liquor dealers or clubs in Leland, he told me about Ruby's Nite Spot, a restaurant, dance hall and gambling club in town that catered to blacks. Ruby Edwards, the former proprietor of the well-known but now closed nightclub, he continued, has been deceased for a number of years. He recalled that Ruby's longtime companion was a high-stakes gambler who traveled around the country, and on more than a few occasions, the man hosted big games at Ruby's club. The games drew large numbers of out-of-state gamblers, he said, including some who drove to Leland from Memphis, St. Louis, Chicago and elsewhere. During the club's heyday, he added, some of the better-known blues musicians played at Ruby's Nite Spot, including Elmore James, Sonny Boy Williamson, B.B. King and many other Delta bluesmen who later became famous. Ruby eventually left Leland to manage Club Ebony in Indianola, and he said that Ruby's daughter, Sue Carroll Hall, met her first husband, B.B. King, at the Indianola club. Although Sue's relationship with King ended, she remarried and later had several children. Currently, Sue lives in Leland and is involved in music, arts and civic activities. The building where Ruby's operated is in poor condition today, but a Mississippi Blues Trail marker, erected in recent years, tells the history of the nightclub.

Chapter 6

Politics, Payola and Raids

Illegal liquor and income from nightclubs and gambling establishments often allowed more than a few men and women to live more comfortable lifestyles than others in the area. Throughout the state, well-off bootleggers and local liquor dealers often flaunted their nouveaux wealth by driving big, expensive cars and sporting flashy clothes and jewelry. One man who grew up in Holmes County in the 1940s recalled that wives and children of area bootleggers and liquor dealers wore more expensive clothes than others in town. But households supported by illegal liquor sales also had more than a few downsides, including domestic violence, failed marriages, prison time and often loss of life.

A thriving liquor business, without the threat of a raid or an arrest, often came with a big price—protection by the county sheriff. Don Drane, who grew up in Holmes County and later lived in the Delta, recalled that elected officials, particularly county sheriffs, appeared to prosper as illegal liquor sales thrived in mid-century Mississippi. He added that "suddenly it seemed the sheriff in every Delta County had a two-story brick house, when the rest of us had white frame houses with asbestos shingles." Tom Givens, who grew up in the Mississippi Delta and now lives out of state, addressed the probability of Delta sheriffs lining their pockets with protection money paid by bootleggers and other liquor dealers when he wrote several years ago about the state's liquor history in an article published online, "Whiskey, Chickens, and Cherry Bombs." The retired administrative law judge also claimed in his article that Head & Jones, a distributing company that operated in the small Delta town of Ruleville, may have been the "largest [illegal liquor] distributor in the entire Southeast United States...Even though liquor consumption was wide open in the Delta and River counties, sales were still basically a local option thing under the supervision of the sheriffs. It's been said most of the Delta sheriffs could have retired for life after two terms, and I have no doubt about that."

BOOGER DEN BOOZE

Not far from Ruleville, Mississippi, in a rather remote and wooded area of Leflore County known as Booger Den, the Whatley brothers allegedly cooked up some of the best moonshine in the state. With a reliable product and a ready market in nearby Delta counties, the brothers often had more customers than they had bottles to fill. The "Den's" location in proximity to two major highways, U.S. 49 and U.S. 82, provided the Whatley brothers and customers easy access to other parts of the Delta and the state. Luster Bayless, who grew up in Ruleville, recalled that Head & Jones, a large wholesale distributor in town, was one of the Whatley brothers' largest customers. Bayless recalled that when he was a young man, he accompanied his father to the Head & Jones store, where large quantities of bonded liquor and moonshine were sold. Bayless recalled Head & Jones sold cases of bonded liquor to nearby liquor dealers, large and small, and the distributor also sold the Whatley brothers' moonshine to customers who requested it. Bayless described the Head & Jones distributorship as a "large warehouse-type store with a counter just inside the door and lots of shelves filled with all types of bonded liquor." The building itself, Bayless explained, was a "Quonset hut–type" structure, similar to the World War II rounded-top metal buildings commonly used on mid-century U.S. military installations. "The old Head & Jones building is still standing," Bayless volunteered and provided the photograph included here.

Bayless also provided the name of a current Ruleville resident, Pete Walker, who once worked as a whiskey runner for the Booger Den moonshine operation. A subsequent contact with Pete Walker revealed that his father, Judge Walker, worked for the Whatley brothers, and he joined his father at work there when he was barely thirteen years old. Pete Walker's primary job was making whiskey runs, delivering Booger Den moonshine to numerous liquor dealers throughout the Delta and

An old building in Ruleville, Mississippi, that was the former location of Head & Jones, an illegal liquor wholesaler. *Courtesy of Luster Bayless.*

northern Mississippi. Walker proudly added that he was never stopped or arrested during his whiskey running days and explained his bailout plan if he had been stopped by law enforcement while transporting a load of moonshine: he planned to burn the old, uninsured family vehicle he drove and its cargo of liquor by igniting a quart jar of gasoline he always carried in the car. And before the vehicle exploded in flames, he planned to roll out the door and run as fast as he could.

Occasionally, Walker recalled, some bootleggers from other counties whose stills had been confiscated or who were under surveillance by their local law enforcement sent runners to Booger Den to pick up supplies of moonshine they intended to resell. Walker added that one particular Holmes County bootlegger, Tillman Branch, who was under scrutiny by Holmes County sheriff Andrew Smith at the time, sent his wife's sister, a woman named Gladys, to Booger Den on more than one occasion to pick up moonshine. Since Tillman's wife, Maxine Ables Branch, had a sister named Gladys Ables, it seems likely that Gladys was the woman Walker mentioned. Although Walker was unable to recall the number of times or exact dates that Gladys drove to Booger Den to pick up moonshine, he specifically remembered the woman because she was "a large woman that wore coveralls and had a short haircut." Walker added that Gladys drove a fairly new Oldsmobile 98, and he remembered the car because he "helped her load it with a hundred or more gallon jars of moonshine" each time she picked up liquor. Conversations Walker had with the woman confirmed the moonshine was intended for Branch's Grocery store in Goodman, Mississippi.

NATIONAL GUARD RAIDS SIMPSON COUNTY

Although sales of illegal liquor were always more concentrated along the Mississippi River, in the Delta and along the Gulf Coast, bootlegging operations and bonded liquor sales existed throughout the state. Less than two months after the National Guard led the much publicized raid on Holmes County nightclubs and liquor dealers on April 1, 1951, a similar action occurred in Simpson County, south of Jackson. Barry M. Stentiford mentioned the event in his book, *The American Home*

Federal officers dumping whiskey down a storm drain on January 15, 1951, in Crystal Springs, Mississippi. *Courtesy of Mississippi Department of Archives and History.*

Federal officers with liquor confiscated during a raid in January 1951 in Crystal Springs. *Courtesy of Mississippi Department of Archives and History.*

Guard: The State Militia in the Twentieth Century, when he stated, "Twelve State guardsmen and thirty-three national guardsmen raided liquor establishments in Simpson County and seized beer, wine, and whiskey, as well as two slot machines."

In subsequent years, the National Guard conducted numerous other liquor and gambling raids throughout the state. Although the official website for the Mississippi National Guard today contains the unit's history in the state of Mississippi, it is interesting to note that these well-chronicled and sometimes controversial raids, ordered by five Mississippi governors over almost three decades, and all of them events involving a tremendous amount of manpower and tax dollars, do not appear in the online document.

RECALLING SHERIFF RUTHERFORD

Illegal liquor and gambling operations continued throughout mid-century Mississippi, and Booneville, in Prentiss County, was one of the better-known northeast Mississippi hot spots. In early 1957, a citizens' group sought help with its county's illegal liquor problems when it complained to Governor J.P. Coleman about Sheriff W.P. Rutherford's failure to close down the county's liquor spots. Subsequently, the governor ordered a National Guard raid overnight on January 12–13, 1957, on Prentiss County cafés and nightspots, and ten individuals were arrested. News accounts of the raid reported a Prentiss County grand jury refused to indict those arrested, and charges against them were dropped after the original search warrant issued by the guardsmen disappeared from the office of the local justice of the peace. District Attorney N.S. Sweatt subsequently sought anti-liquor injunctions against eight Prentiss County establishments owned or operated by R.L Crabb, Eugene Cole, D.L. Winters, Oliver Baggett, Earle Reed, Harold Brinkley, Junior Brinkley and Charles Eaton. Chancellor William Inzer granted six of the injunctions. Finally fed up with the sheriff's lack of enforcement efforts and the unpopular outcome of the local grand jury, a citizens' group known as Prentiss County Citizens' Organization for Law and Order met in Booneville on March 10, 1957, and demanded that Sheriff Rutherford be recalled. *The Delta Democrat-Times* reported that Attorney J.A. Cunningham gave the nearly one thousand people in attendance a choice: "Clean up the county for better law enforcement…or be satisfied and let the bootleggers and gamblers take over." More than one thousand individuals signed a petition to recall the sheriff. Written to Coleman, the petition stated that Rutherford was "in league with the criminal element of the county; that they are thriving under the privilege he allows." *The Delta Democrat-Times* wrote that four out of five districts were "infested with whiskey joints and gambling dens that are run with [Rutherford's] knowledge" and that a grand jury in Prentiss had "failed to hand up indictments against the 10 persons arrested in National Guard raids" because of jury tampering.

Sheriff Rutherford's recall hearing was held in Booneville on June 26, 1957, and a news article published in Greenville's newspaper reported, "Sheriff W.P. Rutherford denied…that he 'sold out' to a criminal element in Prentiss County." Rutherford also testified that he "endeavored to enforce gambling and liquor laws and arrested anyone he knew was violating them," further denying that he "never sold out to anybody." Chancellors J.P. Gillis of Philadelphia, R.P. Sugg of Eupora and William Neville of Meridian heard the case. Allegations against the sheriff apparently split one family down the middle. The news article reported that "J.E. Cunningham, the brother of J.A. Cunningham, who headed the citizens group initiating the petition against the sheriff, testified in Rutherford's defense." Under oath, J.E. Cunningham stated that upon Rutherford's election to the office of sheriff, his brother, J.A. Cunningham, said Rutherford was "a good man and would make a good highway commissioner." J.E. Cunningham's brother later told him that he believed the sheriff had "sold out" to the criminal element in Prentiss County. When questioned about the source of his brother's information, J.E. Cunningham said it came from "one of the criminals" involved in the county's illegal liquor activities. Two other local residents, Reverend Grady Gunthrop, a Baptist minister, and Clovie Bolton, "an automobile dealer whose display windows were smashed during a National Guard raid in the county," also testified during the hearing. The two men stated they had conducted their own investigation of criminal activities in the county, including the sale of illegal liquor, but the news article provided no further details. Of fourteen witnesses, several reported that Governor J.P. Coleman had ordered them to "secretly probe reports of gambling and bootlegging" in Prentiss County over the previous year. Jackson police detective H.A. Stribling testified that he had twice visited the county at the behest of the governor. On his last trip, "he personally bought whiskey from roadhouse operator D.L. Winters." During cross examination, Attorney J.A. Cunningham "admitted that he had 'no direct knowledge' of liquor sales in the county. He said, however, he frequently 'heard' of the illicit trade."

Rutherford appealed the recall decision, but the state court ruled that the election was constitutional based on a 1956 law allowing citizens to remove officials for "willful neglect or failure to perform duties." Subsequently, Sheriff Rutherford's attorneys appealed the lower court's ruling to the Mississippi Supreme Court. On October 26, 1957, and allegedly while Sheriff Rutherford was attending the Ole Miss–Arkansas game in Memphis, forty-six uniformed national guardsmen, ordered into action by Governor Coleman and led by Adjutant General W.P. Wilson, simultaneously raided ten Prentiss County establishments for illegal liquor and gambling activities. The governor's order for the raid was based on additional complaints he had received from Prentiss County citizens that illegal activities still existed in the county. An article published in *The Delta Democrat-Times* two days after the incident reported that fourteen individuals were arrested during the October raid, and seventy cases of whiskey and fifteen gallons of moonshine had been confiscated. Individuals arrested, but free after posting appearance bonds of $200 each, were identified as Oliver J. Brady, R.L. Crabb, J.C. Edge, Herbert Kitchens, T.W. Crowe, Jack Hix, Harold Brinkley, Leon Graham, Charles Eaton, Resse Baggett, Eugene Cole, Grizzard Leach, Aaron Leach and Bonnie Leach. The Greenville newspaper also reported that State Representative H.K. Windham, Sheriff Rutherford's legal counsel, accused Governor Coleman of sending in the troops because he was "mad at the county."

Amazingly, illegal liquor and gambling activities in Prentiss County soon resumed as usual. But in the early summer of 1958, as a result of Sheriff Rutherford's continued failure to enforce the state's laws against liquor and gambling, Governor Coleman ordered another raid on liquor and gambling establishments in the problem-prone northeast county. Focused in Prentiss County, the eighty-four-man brigade raided sixteen establishments, with eleven yielding contraband and eleven of the twenty men arrested charged with possession of illegal liquor. In late 1958, almost two years after Rutherford's appeal was filed, the Mississippi Supreme Court handed down its decision that the state law allowing an elected official to be removed for failure to perform the duties of his office was constitutional. When a recall election was finally held in Prentiss County on April 7, 1959, however, only 2,225 of the county's reported 6,226 registered voters participated in the election. Although 2,106 of those who voted favored a recall, the total vote fell short of the 50 percent needed to remove Sheriff Rutherford from office. A news account of the election's results, published on April 8, 1959, stated that "J.A. Cunningham, Sr., the 86-year old attorney who headed the citizens' group accused Sheriff's forces of 'intimidating, threatening and harassing' voters." Cunningham added, "There is no law or decency in this county, but we aren't licked yet."

LIQUOR AND GAMBLING IN LAUDERDALE COUNTY

Less than a year later, as a result of another citizens' complaint in Lauderdale County, Governor J.P. Coleman ordered the National Guard to carry out a raid on illegal liquor businesses in Meridian, located east of Jackson and very near the Alabama state line. Chancellor William Neville of Meridian signed the complaints, and Major General W.P. Wilson commanded guardsmen who carried out the governor's order. The ten-establishment raid resulted in fourteen individuals charged with illegal possession and confiscation of

$9,000 worth of liquor. *The Delta Democrat-Times* published an Associated Press article describing the weekend raid in its March 2, 1959 edition of the Greenville newspaper:

> *The largest haul came from Three Mile Inn. Officers took about 50 cases of liquor at the place south of [Meridian] on Highway 45 and arrested Robert Blythe and A.J. Lee…Guardsmen found liquor concealed in a basement where the entrance was concealed by a wall panel operated by ropes…They valued their liquor stock at $3,500…Except for a few bottles saved for evidence, all the liquor that contained more than the legal 12 per cent alcohol was smashed by the armed and steel helmeted Guardsmen.*

Alcorn County and the State Line Mob

Years before the National Guard raided the area along U.S. Highway 45 in Lauderdale County, another stretch of the same highway in Alcorn County attracted the attention of local and federal law enforcement. Near the small town of Corinth, just across the line from McNairy County, Tennessee, bootlegging, gambling, prostitution and violence were totally out of hand. Author W.R. Morris, in his 1990 book *The State Line Mob*, wrote that some of the "outlaws settled in the state-line joints when authorities closed the gambling casinos and whorehouses in Phenix City, Alabama." Morris wrote that Jack Hathcock and his wife, Laura Louise Anderson Hathcock, "were the state-line overlords…and operated dives in both Tennessee and Mississippi." Their establishments, Morris added, "thrived on harlots, illegal booze, and shakedown rackets."

The saga of Laura Louise Anderson and Jack Hathcock began in 1937 when they met at the State-Line Club, where Jack worked. After a brief courtship, they were married in Corinth, Mississippi, later that same year. Jack had been raised on a farm in McNairy County by a hard-drinking and often violent father who suffered from "Jake leg," a paralysis-type condition caused by drinking too much rotgut liquor. Even before he was a teenager, Jack picked up spending money by delivering and selling moonshine to kids at his grade school. After his father shot and killed one of Jack's twin brothers, Jack made a quick exit from his parents' household.

During the first two decades of their marriage, Jack and Louise owned and operated four establishments: the State-Line Club, the Forty-Five Grill, built in 1951 after the State-Line Club burned; the Shamrock Restaurant in Mississippi; and the Shamrock Motel, just across the line in McNairy County, Tennessee. Jack built and operated the latter two establishments in 1959, and Louise remained at the Forty-Five Grill. Jack's nephew W.O. Hathcock Jr. and Larice Hathcock, W.O.'s wife, operated the Plantation Club, another liquor and gambling establishment located directly across U.S. Highway 45 from the Forty-Five Grill. Large roadside signs advertising "country ham, red-eye gravy, and homemade biscuits" for forty-five cents lured travelers to the Forty-Five Grill, but Louise's southern cooking, served on red-and-white checkered tablecloths, was only one of several offerings at the roadhouse. With their appetites for food satisfied, many of the male travelers "just passing through" headed to the game room or the dance hall, where liquor, gambling and available women were the main attractions. Most of the men who opted for what they believed to be a quick game of three-card monte or a toss of dice, however, left the place broke and alone. And more likely than not, if the gambler complained too loudly when he lost the last of his cash, or if he threatened to report the Hathcocks' crooked gambling operation to the authorities, he was beaten badly and thrown out the door by Jack and his cohorts. Allegedly, Louise often ended arguments herself when she beat dissatisfied gamblers about the head and shoulders with a ball-peen hammer that she carried in her apron pocket.

Rumors were rampant throughout Alcorn County that more than a few men who had been beaten unconscious after complaining about their gambling losses hadn't made it off the premises. And on several occasions, unrecognizable bodies had floated to the banks of a nearby river. In one situation, a gambler who suffered a major money loss, but left the club alive, stopped in town and filed charges against Jack Hathcock. Before the man left the city limits, however, Jack Hathcock caught up with him and returned his gambling losses. When the man's case came up in court, he failed to appear. A few days later, when the Alcorn County sheriff saw the man at a gas station nearby and asked him why he hadn't appeared in court, he proudly told the sheriff that Jack Hathcock had returned the money he had lost at the club.

The Hathcocks sold large amounts of liquor, allegedly trucked in from a Missouri wholesaler, and much of it was sold and consumed on the premises of the restaurant, clubs and the Shamrock Motel. Local law enforcement conducted frequent raids, but Louise, Jack and their employees were quite adept at hiding large quantities of the liquor inventory outside the roadhouse. Although they were warned in advance before some of the raids, over a period of more than a decade, the Hathcocks were charged with illegal gambling, possession of liquor for resale and possession of illegal weapons. After each arrest, the two individuals readily produced bond money, and local law enforcement soon dismissed the charges. Allegedly, more than a few local residents believed Jack's generous political donations may have kept him and his wife out of jail.

Morris wrote in his book that after one particular raid on the Forty-Five Grill, a deputy sheriff arrived early one morning at the Hathcock home in Corinth to arrest Louise on liquor charges. Since Louise was still in her bathrobe, she asked the deputy to wait while she changed into her work clothes, fixed her hair and applied some makeup. Oddly, the deputy agreed. Once she was dressed for work at the roadhouse, the deputy allowed Louise to drive to the sheriff's office in her own vehicle. Once Louise arrived at the sheriff's office, she quickly posted a $500 bond and made it to work before the lunch crowd arrived.

In 1957, after Louise and Jack had worked as partners for two decades, selling illegal liquor and cheating dozens of restaurant and club patrons out of thousands of dollars each week, Louise decided she wanted a divorce. Louise's primary reason, although unknown to her husband, was that she wanted to spend more time with her lover, a Tallahatchie County–born criminal named Carl Douglas "Towhead" White. The rest of the story of Jack and Louise reads like a B-movie script. Louise divorced Jack; Towhead and Louise conspired to murder Jack; and Towhead shot and killed Jack in a motel room where he was enticed by his wife. Louise convinced authorities she had shot Jack in self-defense and showed bruises to authorities that she had allowed Towhead to inflict on her body. Although Louise was charged with killing Jack in self-defense, it was no surprise when the charges later were dismissed. Louise and Towhead continued their off-and-on relationship, at least when Towhead was in town. The couple never married, in part because Louise saw through Towhead's often obvious attempts to gain control of her money and her business operations.

Almost a decade later, on February 1, 1966, McNairy County sheriff Buford Pusser, in defense, shot and killed Louise Hathcock, the woman many men who knew her had referred to as a "rattlesnake." Louise fired first on Pusser, critically wounding the sheriff, after he attempted to serve her with an arrest warrant at the Shamrock Motel. Minutes before the shooting occurred, Pusser also had confronted Louise with his discovery of a small cache of illegal whiskey in the back of the motel. Ironically, Louise Hathcock died in the same room where she had enticed her ex-husband to his death.

Without a doubt, Louise Hathcock; her husband, Jack; and Towhead White, a repeat offender and frequent visitor to the federal courthouse in Aberdeen, were some of the most infamous members of the State Line Mob. The well-trafficked strip along Highway 45 also was home to a variety of other criminals, including murderers, robbers, bootleggers and others who operated gambling and prostitution rings. Some of the individuals, like Towhead White and a few of his cohorts, including Tommy Bivens and Kirksey McCord Nix Jr., allegedly were affiliated with the Dixie Mafia. Interestingly, Nix, the son of an Oklahoma Criminal Court of Appeals judge of the same name, was a protégé of Mississippi Gulf Coast bar and strip joint owner and reported head of the Dixie Mafia Mike Gillich. For years, it seemed that local law enforcement—including Sheriff Lyle Taylor, County Attorney H.M. Ray, District Attorney N.S. Sweatt and Deputy Sheriffs Earl Mills, R.C. McNair and Grady Bingham, who later served as Alcorn County sheriff—tried but more often failed to prosecute many of these criminals. And it would be years before Alcorn County had seen the last of the State Line Mob.

THE GRANDDADDY OF ALL MOONSHINE RAIDS

Liquor raids, large and small, continued throughout the 1950s and early 1960s across the state, but perhaps the biggest moonshine bust of all happened in Mississippi in early January 1958. Federal agents, sheriff's deputies and various other local law enforcement types participated in a weeklong series of raids throughout the state. An article in the January 14, 1958 edition of *The Delta Democrat-Times* reported on the raid, stating that seventy-nine arrests were made and thirty-four automobiles had been seized. Four local law enforcement officers, including three constables and a former deputy sheriff, were among the individuals arrested on illegal liquor charges. Law enforcement officers arrested and named in the article were Bravo Woodcock, Harrison County Beat 3, Pass Christian; Clifton Saucier of Standard, in Hancock County; and Herschel Landrum, Forrest County constable at Brooklyn, Mississippi. Lewis West, supervisor of Alcohol Tax Unit agents for Mississippi, said Landrum was expected to be charged with bribing another officer. Interestingly, John Pettus, who was arrested on April 1, 1951, during Operation Blackjack in Holmes County, was among the individuals named in the news article.

Undercover Agent Revealed

A fascinating aspect of this large-scale raid netting several dozen arrests was the role played by Thomas "Tommy" Stewart, a twenty-seven-year-old undercover agent who worked for the Federal Alcohol Tax Unit office in Jackson. During his interview with a United Press International (UPI) correspondent, Stewart said he accepted the undercover assignment in June 1957 and successfully infiltrated several large moonshine operations in the six-month period leading up to the raid. The news account reported that Steward "posed as a bootlegger and a fugitive from justice to win the confidence of the bootleggers. He said he was threatened by a man he described as a 'kingpin' of the bootlegging industry in Mississippi...the man said he would kill me when he got out of the penitentiary." Eventually, Stewart worked for James Crump of Tupelo, one of the area's largest suppliers. While in his employ, Stewart estimated that a bootlegger could make $125,000 a year and that the wholesale price was from $2.50 to $3.00 per gallon, with most moonshine transported by car in 225-gallon amounts. Stewart's account of his undercover experiences was further detailed in the UPI article:

> *I started out on a small scale in North Mississippi getting acquainted with the small time operators. Then I drifted down on the coast and hung around the joints known to be frequented by the larger operators. I gradually got acquainted with them. I led them to believe I was on the wanted list in Alabama and had to drift around. They gradually accepted me as a bootlegger... The public thinks the moonshiner is a little fellow out on his farm with a couple of barrels making a little drinking whiskey but this is big business. [Bootleggers] were involved in all sorts of crime. They propositioned me about joining a stolen automobile ring and a narcotics ring. They have a cold and evil way of talking all their own.*

Chapter 7

The Black Market Tax

In 1908, the Mississippi legislature enacted statewide prohibition of alcohol, and the law became effective on January 1, 1909. In spite of the state's law, the sale of illegal liquor, over time, became a multimillion-dollar business, and the bootleggers and illegal liquor dealers kept the untaxed profits for themselves. But in 1944, after state legislators reached the consensus that Mississippi was losing money by not collecting taxes on large amounts of revenue generated by illegal liquor sales, the legislature enacted what was called a black market tax law. Although lawmakers presented the tax to their constituencies as an effort to limit sales of certain rationed items during World War II (tires, sugar, coffee, cigarettes, etc.) and as a method of returning revenue to the state treasury, most residents believed the legislation's primary intent was to collect taxes on previously untaxed illegal liquor. The new law allowed the state to levy and collect a 10 percent tax, and it delegated enforcement authority to the tax collector's office. Additionally, the law gave the state legal authority to spend tax revenues collected. A rather unique portion of the black market tax law allowed the state tax collector to keep 10 percent of tax monies collected for himself.

The tax, of course, was an unpopular one, and in the years that followed, a number of taxpayers challenged its validity by filing lawsuits against the state. One of these lawsuits involved Edna Bishop, who had been convicted of selling illegal liquor in her south Mississippi restaurant. In November 1950, the Mississippi Supreme Court issued a decision on an appeal filed on Bishop's behalf, and a United Press article reported the high court's findings in the November 13, 1950 edition of *The Delta Democrat-Times*. Written by Harold Foreman, the article was published under the headline "High Court Rules the Tax Collector Must Get Hypocrite Tax." Foreman reported the high court did not rule on the legality of the state's black market tax, although it stated a tax collector could employ "every remedy available for the collection of the tax." In its decision, however, the court upheld the state's right to collect tax on liquor sales despite being dry, calling it "neither immoral nor discriminatory." The opinion was handed down as a result of an appeal on Edna Bishop's liquor conviction for selling alcohol at Edna's Kitchen, a business she operated near Laurel. Mrs. Bishop had appealed on the grounds that collection of the 10 percent black market tax was allegedly the real motive behind her arrest. The opinion also upheld similar convictions against Dewey Loftin and E.C. "Lige" Holifield.

THE TAX COLLECTOR

In 1956, incumbent state tax collector Nellah Bailey, widow of former Mississippi governor Thomas L. Bailey, died after serving three terms. After Mrs. Bailey's death, Governor J.P. Coleman appointed Mississippi state legislator William F. Winter to fill her unexpired term. Winter's appointment to the office of state tax collector occurred soon after his failed election attempt to unseat Speaker of the House Walter Sillers. More than a few individuals watching from the sidelines believed Governor Coleman's appointment was a consolation prize of sorts for Winter. The rumor apparently stemmed from the fact that Governor Coleman had supported Sillers, not Winter, in the race for the Speaker's position. Regardless of the reason behind his appointment, Winter was handed a golden opportunity to make more money than the governor's salary at the time, $15,000 per year. When Winter assumed the tax collector position, various news accounts estimated that approximately one thousand wholesale and retail liquor establishments operated in fifty-one of the eighty-two counties in the legally dry state of Mississippi. The majority of these businesses, however, were situated in eleven counties that bordered the Mississippi River and in the three counties along the Gulf Coast. Approximately three hundred of the establishments were in Harrison County, where the beachfront resort towns of Gulfport and Biloxi were located. Winter's biographer, Charles C. Bolton, detailed the former governor and state tax collector's concerns about his appointed position. Because of the importance of the revenue produced by the black market tax, Winter thought it "should be retained as long as official prohibition remained." He believed, however, that a more efficient method of collecting the tax existed: abolish the tax collector's office and merge its duties with those of the Mississippi State Tax Commission. The recommendation gained no traction during the 1958 session in part because the head of the state tax commission, Noel Monaghan, lobbied against the proposal and "disliked the black market tax and wanted nothing to do with collecting the funds."

A Political Hot Potato

Monaghan was not the only public official who wanted to maintain an arm's-length relationship with the tax on illegal alcohol. More than a few legislators were concerned that any discussions about the black market tax would trigger political discussions concerning the validity of taxing an illegal item. In 1959, with his term expiring that year, Winter declared himself an official candidate for the position he had occupied since 1956. Almost immediately, nine candidates signed up to run against him. An article written by Charles C. Bolton and published in the *Journal of Mississippi History* speculated that the number of Winter's challengers in the election may have been determined by the earning potential of the tax collector, basing his belief on the "record amount of revenue, almost 1.3 million dollars," that the office collected in 1958 alone. Bolton suggested a second reason for the large number of opposing candidates could be explained by common knowledge that Winter had successfully resisted membership in the White Citizens' Council. Armed with name recognition as a former legislator, the availability of campaign funds and recent experience already garnered from serving as tax collector, Winter easily won the election for another four-year term in office.

In the years that followed, Winter's salary and the large commissions he received on tax monies collected became the subject of controversy not only in Mississippi but nationally as well. An article written by Norman Ritter and published in the May 11, 1962 edition of *Life* magazine reported that during 1961, Winter collected approximately $1.45 million in taxes on illegal liquor. The article also reported Winter's share of the tax revenues was $145,000, a hefty figure for the early 1960s, especially when the U.S. president earned an annual salary of $100,000, plus $50,000 in expenses, and Mississippi's governor received only $25,000. In recent years, former administrative law judge Thomas Givens wrote about Winter's lucrative job as Mississippi's black market tax collector. "Now, get this," he wrote. "They had a 'State Tax Collector.' His only job was to collect the black market tax, and his compensation was a percentage of the collection. In the 50's, *Life* magazine did a profile on him as the highest paid public servant in the United States. That was none other than the most Honorable William Winter."

On May 15, 1962, Connellsville, Pennsylvania's *Daily Courier* reported that the "Senate Monday joined the House in overwhelmingly approving a bill to abolish the tax collector's office Jan. 1, 1964, when Winter's four-year term expires." The cancellation of the $65,000-a-year job marked the beginning of the end of Mississippi's black market tax. "I think I held the office as long as a reasonable man should want to hold such a high-paying public position," said Winter. The newspaper article referenced may have underreported the total amount of money Winter allegedly received during the seven years he collected black market taxes in Mississippi. By most accounts, his state-mandated "commission" of 10 percent amounted to slightly over $1 million.

WINTER'S VISIT TO VICKSBURG

During a video of a book talk made by Winter while promoting Bolton's biography, he acknowledged that about one hundred wholesale liquor dealers operated in Mississippi during the seven years he served as tax collector. The former legislator, tax collector and Mississippi governor stated that liquor was legal in Louisiana, just across the Mississippi River from Vicksburg, and that Louisiana dealers regularly sold liquor to Mississippi wholesalers. He further explained an agreement between the tax collector's office and liquor dealers in Louisiana, requiring Louisiana liquor dealers to provide his office with copies of invoices for all inventory sold to Mississippi wholesalers. Three of his state's wholesalers, Winter said, were located close to one another on Washington Street in Vicksburg. Winter recalled that he visited these distributors shortly after a severe tornado hit Vicksburg, wreaking havoc on the downtown area. One of the wholesale distributors he visited had suffered tremendous wind damage, and much of the company's liquor inventory had been destroyed. Although Winter did not identify the Vicksburg wholesalers by names, it seems reasonable to believe that Delta Distributing Company, mentioned later in this book, was one of the three wholesale liquor dealers that Winter visited in the aftermath of the storm.

"We Pay Liquor Tax"

Although the black market tax was abolished effective January 1, 1964, by most accounts, Mississippi was still taking in about $4.5 million in liquor tax from an estimated total of $36 million in liquor sales per year. Over 1,700 liquor retailers and 18 wholesale liquor dealers had been licensed by the state, and all were taxed on a substance that was illegal in a state with a law in place for more than five decades. Owners and operators of restaurants, service stations and other businesses often displayed printed signs bearing the message, "We pay state liquor tax." Although liquor sales were illegal, many who sold liquor seemed unafraid to publicly, even proudly, advertise that they paid tax on illegal liquor sales. Shortly after Governor Paul B. Johnson Jr. was sworn in in January 1964, the state's long-standing liquor issue, including taxes paid on the illegal substance, rose to the forefront of Mississippi politics. Barely six months later, on June 3, 1964, *The Delta Democrat-Times* reported that members of the Mississippi House of Representatives had voted 87–16 on a new tax bill passed the previous day. The article quoted several lawmakers, including Representative Roy Thigpen, who had "handled the bills on the floor." Thigpen stated, "The State Tax Commission envisioned making about a 16 percent profit in its task as the state's exclusive liquor wholesaler." State Representative Walter Phillips, of Hancock County, west of Biloxi, one of the individuals who shepherded the proposed legislation to its passage, said he voted against the bill. Phillips explained his decision by stating, "The proposed license fees were so high they would lead to bootlegging in his county."

On July 22, 2014, an article entitled "'Black Market' Illegal Liquor Tax Was Hidden Away at the Capitol," written by lobbyist Donna Echols, appeared in the *Clarion-Ledger*, Jackson's longtime newspaper. The article primarily included the history, design and architecture of Mississippi's New Capitol Building, now a state museum, but it also profiled one of the historic building's lesser-known features: a Mosler-designed and built safe or "vault," as it had been identified in years past. Custom built on the second floor

An old Mosler safe pictured before the renovation of the New State Capitol Building, Jackson, Mississippi. *Courtesy of Mississippi Department of Archives and History.*

of Mississippi's New Capitol Building, the vault dates back to 1903 and is original to the building. Allegedly, at one time, the safe was the repository for tax monies collected on illegal liquor sales.

Chapter 8

Mississippi Liquor
Wholesalers

Moonshine was easy to find during Mississippi's prohibition days, but bonded liquor was readily available for purchase as well. By most accounts, bonded liquor most often was brought into Mississippi by either boat or rail and driven to its final destination. Distributors of very large quantities of illegal liquor usually maintained warehouses near the shipping point, and liquor dealers or individuals called "whiskey runners" hauled the liquor away in trucks frequently disguised to hide their precious cargos.

Willie Mae Bradshaw, the daughter of infamous bootlegger G.W. "Red" Hydrick, believed her father may have been one of the largest distributors of illegal liquor in mid-century Mississippi. In her father's biography, *Big Red*, Bradshaw shared the story of one of many liquor runs her father and his men allegedly made between Vicksburg and Rankin County. During the trip along U.S. Highway 80, Hydrick and his companions followed the truckload of liquor they had just picked up at a Vicksburg warehouse. After they crossed from Warren County into Hinds County, both Hydrick and the truck driver observed what each believed to be a Hinds County deputy sheriff's car. The truck driver immediately turned off his headlights, left the highway and quickly abandoned the vehicle in nearby woods. Hydrick also turned off his headlights, pulled the car just off the roadway and waited for the truck's driver to run back to the car. The driver soon located the car and jumped inside, and Hydrick sped away. Anticipating a stop by the sheriff's deputy, one of the men riding with Hydrick opened a bottle of whiskey that the men passed around and took drinks from, and then they poured the remainder of the bottle on their clothes to make it appear they had been drinking. When the deputy caught up with Hydrick's car and pulled him over, he found a carful of men who reeked of booze. Convinced the men in the car were drunk, the lawman let them go. Bradshaw wrote that her father and some of his men returned to the scene the next day and recovered the truck loaded with liquor.

Red Hydrick's nephew Ken Hydrick Flessas recalled the dependence of East Jackson clubs on Vicksburg's ready supply of liquor, stating, "Vicksburg was one of those 'distribution centers' the Clubs in East Jackson depended on to keep their stock of booze full. My cousin [Red Hydrick's son] used to make that haul quite frequently. The highway patrol knew each vehicle that came there for pick ups, they turned a blind eye to what was going on." Another individual who remembered Vicksburg's involvement in the state's illegal liquor traffic was Gene Harlan Powell, the author of *Fisher of Men: The Motorcycle Ministry of Herb Shreve*. Powell grew up in Yazoo City, not too distant from Vicksburg. As a young man, Powell and a friend once accompanied a Yazoo City restaurant manager they knew on one of his liquor runs to Vicksburg. Powell stated, "Loyd Price, the manager of the Tenderloin Grill [Four Points intersection] in Yazoo City, used to make runs to Vicksburg late [after closing the restaurant]. He would go to the liquor store on Levee St. in Vicksburg and load the trunk of his car with bonded whiskey. 'Sonny' Berry and I rode over there with him one night back in 1953." It seems in mid-century Mississippi, where illegal liquor was concerned, all roads ran to Vicksburg.

Over in Holmes County, Bluford Taylor and his brother, Percy Paul Taylor, were among the largest suppliers of bonded liquor in the Mississippi Delta and possibly in the hills of north central Mississippi. The Taylor brothers, as they were known to locals, operated a well-known store and juke joint in Tchula. By most accounts, the Taylor brothers also maintained a large warehouse in Lexington, the county seat of Holmes County. Jimmy Dale Branch, bootlegger Tillman Branch's youngest son, recalled a trip he made as a teenager with men who worked for his father to Lexington, where they picked up bonded liquor for the Blue Flame and for Branch's Grocery. He added that some of Tillman's patrons preferred bonded liquor over moonshine, the "house drink" at his father's nightclubs. The liquor warehouse in Lexington, Branch explained, was "a huge place" where "hundreds of cases" of bonded liquor were stored. After a local option law was passed and Holmes County voted wet, Percy Paul Taylor Sr. opened a package store in Tchula, where he often worked alone. Ironically, during a robbery of the legal liquor store, the man who had spent most of his adult life illegally selling liquor in what many remember as a lawless and extremely dangerous environment was shot and killed. In later years, Bluford Taylor operated a supermarket in Lexington, and his lengthy obituary published in the *Holmes County Herald* indicated that the former bootlegger was a service-minded citizen who lived until he was eighty-three years old.

Throughout the 1950s, the Taylor brothers endured years of stiff competition from several other distributors in the Vicksburg and Delta region, including one alleged wholesaler in adjacent Leflore County. A distant cousin of mine, Jim H. Branch, who grew up in the Greenwood area, remembered a large distributing company operated by the Malouf family and located in his hometown of Greenwood, the seat of Leflore County. Headed by patriarch Foad Malouf, the distributor allegedly sold bonded liquor to local dealers for resale in their restaurants, stores and nightclubs. Jim Branch recalled that his uncle, Max Branch, the proprietor of a Sidon, Mississippi grocery store, was among the Greenwood distributor's regular customers. Interestingly, Max Branch was a great-nephew of Holmes County bootlegger Tillman Branch, also a distant cousin of mine and the subject of the book entitled *The Juke Joint King of the Mississippi Hills*. Like other small grocery stores in business during state prohibition, Branch sold food, sundries and other necessary items that filled the store's floor-to-ceiling shelves. Along with the usual household merchandise, Max Branch also maintained a large inventory of illegal bonded liquor. Jim Branch explained that his great-uncle stored the bottles of liquor underneath the counter, where they were out of sight to customers and visible only to the store's clerks. Jim added that Max also offered slot machines, located in the back of the store, for his customers' gambling pleasure. Gambling, like liquor, was also illegal.

Jim Branch vividly recalled an incident in which he was involved with illegal slot machines. The event occurred during one of the teenage summers he spent in the early 1960s with his grandparents in Sidon. His uncle Max asked him to go to Greenwood with some men who worked around the store to help the men load several slot machines they planned to transport back to the Sidon store. Branch recalled the trip well, since the road from Sidon to Greenwood and back was a bumpy, dusty gravel one. While one of the men drove the truck, Jim's job was to help the other men keep watch over the slot machines in the back to ensure they arrived in Sidon in good condition. The gambling devices, Jim said, were hidden from view with a large tarpaulin. As the truck's driver navigated the vehicle with its heavy load along the rough road, an unexpected large gust of wind blew the tarpaulin off, revealing the slot machines in the bed of the truck. Branch recalled how frightened

A typical 1940s slot machine. *Courtesy of Wikipedia Commons, photo by Valerie Everett.*

and concerned he was about being arrested if law enforcement happened along while they retrieved the tarpaulin and recovered the slot machines. Fortunately, Jim said, no one else observed the incident.

During state prohibition, liquor distributors, grocery stores, nightclubs, juke joints and other places selling illegal liquor flourished because the public's demand for alcohol was so strong. But the real success of an illegal liquor operation, in addition to a steady stream of cash-paying customers, often depended on the protection of local law enforcement officers who looked the other way in exchange for money or favors. Ironically, Max Branch's brother Benjamin Harrison "Ben" Branch Jr., was a longtime officer on the Greenwood police force before he retired in the 1970s.

Mike Morrissey and Delta Distributing Company

Delta Distributing Company, located in Warren County in the historic Mississippi river port town of Vicksburg, may have been the largest wholesale liquor distributor in the entire state of Mississippi. Historical court records establish that the distributing company, located on Washington Street near downtown Vicksburg, imported liquor from Louisiana, where liquor was sold legally, and illegally resold it to dealers in Mississippi. Revealing details about Delta Distributing Company's involvement in the illegal liquor business in mid-century Mississippi are contained in a Mississippi Supreme Court decision handed down on October 10, 1960. Mike T. Morrissey, a Vicksburg businessman and one of the alleged owners of Delta Distributing Company, filed the original lawsuit against Giuseppe Bologna, a Louisiana liquor dealer to whom he owed money. (See *240 Miss. 284 (1960) 123 So. 2d 537, Morrissey v. Bologna, et al.*) A review of the Mississippi Supreme Court's 1960 decision confirmed that Delta Distributing Company was, in fact, engaged in the business of buying illegal liquor from at least one out-of-state distributor, Bologna Brothers, for resale to Morrissey's Mississippi customers.

Morrissey was no stranger to lawsuits. On December 3, 1953, he had been sued by W.J. Vollar, Landman Teller and James P. Biedenharn, of the law firm Vollar, Teller and Biedenharn in Vicksburg, for nonpayment of outstanding legal fees incurred during their representation of Morrissey in an Internal Revenue Service compromise-settlement agreement. The background of that lawsuit was included in a decision rendered by the

The rail bridge across the Mississippi River at Vicksburg, with the U.S. Highway 80 Auto Bridge located to the left. *Courtesy of Wikipedia Commons, photo by Rob Shenk.*

Mississippi Supreme Court on February 7, 1955, stating the intent of the original suit was to "recover an alleged balance of $10,500 on a fee of $22,500 for legal services rendered in connection with the compromise and settlement of a claim...for delinquent income taxes." Total taxes owed amounted to $267,278 and covered a period of six or more years, beginning in 1942. The suit was complicated and involved threats of criminal prosecution against Morrissey regarding the amounts of income he had reported. Paramount to the issue was controversy about the actual ownership of Delta Distributing Company, and it was questioned whether Morrissey was sole owner or whether Steve Castleman, the reputed owner, paid him a salary. The latter claim was later denied.

Instruments in the court's possession in the case of *Morrissey v. Bologna, et al,* filed on October 8, 1958, established that Mike T. Morrissey, as the owner of Delta Distributing Company, purchased liquor from a wholesale business owned by Giuseppe Bologna. The business relationship between Morrissey and Bologna was a simple one. Bologna's operation was located in Baton Rouge, Louisiana, where the sale of liquor was legal, and he sold liquor to Morrissey for resale in Mississippi, where it was illegal. Although the original court case and the subsequent Mississippi Supreme Court decision rendered on October 10, 1960, peripherally involved the transfer of ownership of two Warren County real estate parcels, Southall Place and Grey Oaks, from Morrissey's wife, Elizabeth, to her husband for use as collateral for debts owed Bologna, the facts in the case reveal some intimate details about the purchase and resale of illegal liquor in mid-century Mississippi. Based on detailed records referenced in court documents, its seems that Delta Distributing Company likely was the source of large quantities of bonded liquor sold to liquor dealers, nightclubs and juke joints near Vicksburg.

Captain Tom Morrissey

Michael T. Morrissey's involvement with illegal liquor actually began with his father, Captain Thomas Michael Morrissey, an Irish immigrant who married his Vicksburg-area wife, Josephine Romano, the daughter of Sam Romano, born in Salerno, Italy. After settling in Vicksburg, Morrissey opened a bar on some docking space on the Louisiana side of the Yazoo Canal that could be reached by Mississippi customers by boat. Eventually, the bar evolved into a nightclub, complete with gambling, food and entertainment. Morrissey's empire grew, and he purchased land on the Louisiana side to maintain a monopoly of whiskey sales to Mississippi. "He always carried a pistol with him in the car," wrote Morrissey's grandson. "He had numerous friends and according to my mother controlled politics in Vicksburg for a number of years. It was always to his advantage for Vicksburg to be dry."

Without a doubt, Mike Morrissey's connections to those who bought and sold illegal liquor ran deep along the Mississippi River corridor, and available documents indicate that his business relationship with Bologna Brothers of Louisiana extended over a period of almost a decade. Evidence of the long-standing relationship appeared in the text of the Mississippi Supreme Court's decision. Mike Morrissey died on February 20, 1960, almost eight months before the high court decided his debt to Giuseppe Bologna was null and void. The court's decision provided details of Bologna's relationship to Mike T. Morrissey, including Bologna's own admission while testifying as an adverse witness that he had been selling liquor since 1946 to Mike Morrissey, who operated as Delta Distributing Company in Vicksburg, Mississippi. Bologna's place of business, he claimed, was in Baton Rouge, Louisiana, but he traveled back and forth to Vicksburg to "confer with Morrissey, that bills of lading for the shipments were made to Vicksburg and the liquor was sold

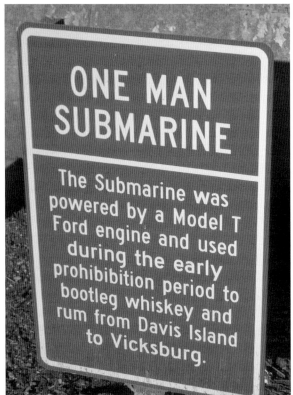

Above: A one-man bootlegger submarine used during prohibition to smuggle liquor from Davis Island to Vicksburg, Mississippi. *Courtesy of Grand Gulf Military Park, Port Gibson, Mississippi.*

Left: A sign describing the one-man bootlegger submarine on display at Grand Gulf Military Park. *Courtesy of Grand Gulf Military Park, Port Gibson, Mississippi.*

A thirty-seven-foot bootlegger canoe carved from Tupelo gum suspended from the ceiling at the Museum of the Mississippi Delta, Greenwood, Mississippi. *Courtesy of Cheryl A. Taylor.*

to Morrissey in Mississippi; he knew that Morrissey was selling this liquor in Mississippi; the notes and deeds of trust involved in this litigation were given as security for Morrissey's purchases of Liquor; he knew...the sale of liquor in Mississippi was illegal; he had been in Morrissey's place of business about fifty times, and, on occasions, had made collections while there; and the notes and deeds of trust were executed and delivered in Mississippi." The court's decision cited Section 2612, Code of 1942, Recompiled, which provided, "If any person shall trust or give credit to another for intoxicating liquor, he shall lose the debt, and be forever disabled from recovering the same or any part thereof; and all notes or securities given therefor, under whatever pretense, shall be void." In summary, the decision stated, "Bologna lost his debt, and his notes and deeds of trust were void...In law, he was not even a creditor."

The Bologna Brothers Fight Back in Court

The legal fight to recover the debts owed by Morrissey to Bologna, however, did not end with the Mississippi Supreme Court decision in 1960. Instead, the decision denying validity of debts owed by Morrissey to Bologna became the basis of a lawsuit filed by Bologna Brothers, et al, against Mike T. Morrissey, deceased, and Elizabeth M. Morrissey, et al, seeking the recovery of monies owed from Morrissey's estate. The background of the lawsuit, contained in a decision rendered on May 21, 1963, by the Louisiana Court of Appeals, stated the suit "arose out of business transactions between Bologna Brothers, a Louisiana partnership engaged in the State of Louisiana in selling whiskey at wholesale, and Mike T. Morrissey, engaged in the business of selling whiskey in the City of Vicksburg, Mississippi." The appeal was filed in Madison Parish, Louisiana, where property owned by the late Mike Morrissey and his wife, Elizabeth, and secured by promissory notes given to Bologna by Morrissey before his death, was located. The text of the decision stated, "Mike T. Morrissey died on February 20, 1960, and his legal heirs were substituted as defendants in the lawsuit." In December 1953, Morrissey had purchased whiskey valued at $75,000 from the plaintiffs, who sold liquor from their wholesale establishments in Baton Rouge and in Bogalusa, Louisiana, and on December 22, 23 and 29, 1953, Morrissey's driver, "Melvin Fendley...authorized by Morrissey under power of attorney to sign invoices, accept deliveries and act for and on behalf of his principal in securing and transporting liquor to Vicksburg," was present when the whiskey was placed in Morrissey's truck in Baton Rouge "for the purpose of being transported to Morrissey's place of business in Vicksburg." On each of the three days that Fendley transported liquor from Baton Rouge to Vicksburg, a Louisiana Department of Revenue representative witnessed the loading of Morrissey's truck and "issued an export transportation permit to Morrissey, permitting his driver, Fendley, to transport the merchandise...to Morrissey's premises in Vicksburg." Louisiana statutes stated that "such exported beverages were not subject to the Louisiana tax." On January 22, 1954, after deliveries had been made to Vicksburg, Morrissey requested that Leo Boolas, a certified public accountant in Vicksburg, draw up ten promissory notes in the amount of $5,000 each. Elizabeth M. and Mike T. Morrissey, co-makers, signed the notes that were payable at one-year intervals to Bologna Brothers at the Merchants National Bank & Trust Company in Vicksburg.

Ultimately, the Louisiana Court of Appeals held that Mississippi courts, for "reasons of public policy," refused to aid creditors who sought "to recover on a note given as evidence of a debt for intoxicating liquors, not because the note is void, but because the courts will not aid a person who founds his cause of action upon his own immoral or illegal act. The notes are not essentially invalid, they are simply non-enforceable in a Mississippi court."

The court further stated it was unaware of Louisiana law or "consideration of public policy" that would prevent the plaintiff's recovery on the notes and determined a judgment was "correct in its determination of [Morrissey's heirs] liabilities for their father's debt."

Chapter 9

The Gold Coast of Rankin County

About fifty miles east of Vicksburg, just across the Pearl River from Mississippi's capital city of Jackson, lies a sparsely populated and flood-prone portion of Rankin County where illegal liquor thrived for over three decades. Sometime in the early to mid-1930s, illegal gambling and liquor spots sprang up in the area that some called "East Jackson" and others referred to simply as "'cross the river." As businesses grew and money rolled in, the area became known as the "Gold Coast." From the mid-'30s until the early '60s, dozens of nightclubs and restaurants selling illegal liquor operated along Casey's Lane and Old Fannin Road, now part of Rankin County's bustling development. Along with illegal liquor, many of these establishments offered gambling that ranged from wagering on cockfights and dog fights to slot machines, dice and blackjack. Some individuals who are old enough to remember the area recall that prostitution thrived, as well, in a few of the run-down motels and in the back rooms of some nightspots. Across the Pearl River in Jackson and in the surrounding area, citizens who opposed alcohol and the activities that followed its sale and consumption often referred to this portion of Rankin County as "Sin City." One early blues singer, Armenter Chatmon, better known as Bo Carter, memorialized East Jackson and its nightlife activities in his "East Jackson Blues," recorded in 1928 on the Brunswick label. Carter was most well known for performing on stage and for recordings he made with his brothers, Sam Chatmon and Lonnie Chatmon, and their friend Walter Vinson when they performed as the Mississippi Sheiks.

A view of downtown Jackson, circa 1935. *Courtesy of Mississippi Department of Archives and History.*

A MUD HOLLOW MONTE CARLO

Prior to 1934, the only business activities at the crossroads of U.S. Highway 80 East and U.S. Highway 49 South were "gas filling stations, a couple of hot dog stands, and a half-dozen corn-liquor peddlers." In 1934, however, a man named Pat Hudson set up an illegal gambling establishment near the junction of these two most traveled highways in Mississippi, hoping to make some fast cash. Shortly after Hudson set up his gambling operation, a man named Sam Seaney set up shop nearby. By most accounts, Seaney had a similar idea—he believed the perfect location near the intersection of two major highways, selling illegal liquor and offering a few games of chance made a winning combination for getting rich quick. Other information about Seaney indicates it may have been his daytime job at a Rankin County sawmill and creosote operation that drove him to find an easier, cleaner and better-paying way of making a living. A listing in a Jackson City Directory published in 1930 indicated that Seaney and his wife, Zelphia, lived at 418

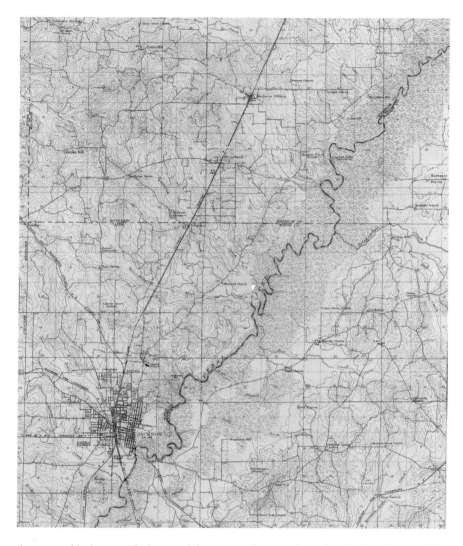

A topographical map of Jackson and the surrounding area, including Rankin County, 1905. *University of Texas Library Maps (online).*

East Gulfport Road in East Jackson. A notation in the directory listing indicated that Seaney operated a business at the location and identified it as Jeep Tourist Court. Seaney's parents, Alex A. and Minnie Seaney, lived in a residence at 820 Casey's Lane, and Seaney's brother Eugene and his wife, May, lived a few blocks away at 512 Casey's Lane. Interestingly, Casey's Lane and Fannin Road were the two primary streets in Rankin County identified in later years as East Jackson. Today, a Mississippi Blues Trail marker constructed nearby identifies the location of the early Gold Coast entertainment district.

After Hudson and Seaney established their liquor and gambling operations near the busy intersection, word quickly spread that money was to be made in Rankin County. Soon, would-be businessmen from larger cities, including Chicago, Memphis, St. Louis and New Orleans, arrived with competition on their minds and dollar signs in their eyes. One of these individuals, J.H. "Doc" Steed, a Hot Springs, Arkansas man who had served time in a federal penitentiary on a narcotics charge, was among these early individuals who set up liquor and gambling operations in the area that became the Gold Coast. Steed opened a business near the foot of the bridge over the Pearl River, a club he named the Blue Peacock, believing the club's location was the perfect place to attract patrons from downtown Jackson as they drove by his place each day on their way home from work. But a big problem existed in Rankin County—the Pearl River flooded each spring, and restaurant and club owners soon found that building in flood-prone Rankin County, especially near the foot of the bridge spanning the culprit river, wasn't a good idea. Very soon, club operators and liquor dealers discovered that their restaurants and nightclubs, often simple wooden structures, simply could not survive Rankin County's annual floods. Structures built above the ground on so-called stilts often were the only buildings to survive the Pearl River's floodwaters. More often than not, club owners found themselves rebuilding after the floodwaters receded, but the muddy streets and parking areas left behind caused some who visited the Gold Coast to refer to it as a "Mud Hollow Monte Carlo." To make the situation even worse, these dark, muddy parking lots frequently became the scene of brawls, stabbings and shootings.

The Rankin County sheriff's office had its hands full in keeping law and order on the Gold Coast. After J.V. Therrell was elected sheriff in 1932, raids on Gold Coast liquor and gambling establishments became commonplace. But as soon as Therrell attempted to clean up one joint, another sprang up. During one of these raids, someone hit Sheriff Therrell over the head with a beer bottle and knocked him unconscious. While the sheriff spent several weeks in a local hospital recovering from his injuries, he contemplated whether he should run for reelection.

Rankin County law enforcement changed hands in 1936, when T.B. Spann was elected to serve the county as sheriff. During Sheriff Spann's first year in office, Governor Hugh White traveled across the Pearl River to the Gold Coast in response to complaints from a group of Rankin County

The Woodrow Wilson Bridge over Pearl River under construction. *Courtesy of Mississippi Department of Archives and History.*

The Woodrow Wilson Memorial Bridge, linking Jackson to Rankin County, the day after opening in January 1941. *Courtesy of Mississippi Department of Archives and History.*

citizens about illegal liquor and gambling. One of the individuals signing the complaint was N.S. Jackson, head of the Anti-Saloon League of Jackson. An Associated Press article published on September 12, 1936, in Biloxi's

Pearl River floodwaters under the Woodrow Wilson Bridge. *Courtesy of Mississippi Department of Archives and History.*

Daily Herald reported that the governor "personally visited the suburban section and promised to call out the state soldiery" if the illegal activities continued. The governor added that he had received "letters from 200 mothers in Jackson appealing to me on behalf of their sons and daughters to do something about this situation," and he pledged to provide Sheriff Spann "whatever assistance he needs." The following year, Governor White made good on his promise and ordered the National Guard to conduct a large-scale raid on Rankin County's illegal operations. On November 9, 1937, sixty-eight guardsmen, commanded by Major T.B. Birdsong, conducted the operation and confiscated large quantities of bonded liquor. Gambling equipment and paraphernalia were destroyed, and several individuals were arrested during the raid.

In the aftermath of the November raid, District Attorney Percy Lee filed a complaint against Guysell McPhail and others who were seeking injunctions to remove padlocks on their nightclubs closed during the raid. An Associated Press article published a few weeks later in the *Daily Herald* reported, "The complaint [against the injunction] alleged possession of gambling paraphernalia and was based on evidence gathered by the guardsmen." Chancellor A.B. Amis of Meridian dismissed the district attorney's complaint, stating that the use of sixty-eight national guardsmen as peace officers in the raid was "illegal" and was "headed for the Mississippi Supreme Court." In his opinion, Chancellor Amis said the governor's authority to use the National Guard was "strictly limited" and "strikes at the very foundation of our republican form of government." The chancellor's decision was appealed to the Mississippi Supreme Court, which requested a decision on the legality of Governor White's order for the National Guard to raid Rankin County liquor and gambling establishments. During its March 1938 term, the state Supreme Court rendered a decision in the matter of the *State v. McPhail*, upholding the constitutionality of the governor's order to the National Guard to raid Gold Coast nightspots the year before. With the high court's decision on record, Governor White and several other governors who served in later years, including Paul B. Johnson, Fielding Wright, J.P. Coleman, Ross Barnett and Paul B. Johnson Jr., issued numerous executive

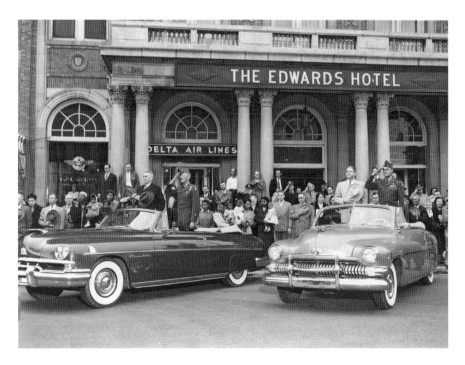

Governor White, Mayor Thompson and National Guard officers at the Edwards Hotel in downtown Jackson, 1951. *Courtesy of Mississippi Department of Archives and History.*

orders to the National Guard to conduct raids aimed at enforcing state prohibition and gambling laws in Mississippi. Historical documents indicate that Governor White alone ordered over a dozen raids on Gold Coast establishments between 1937 and 1939.

LIQUOR DEALERS, EX-CONS AND THE LAW

The Blue Peacock's owner, Doc Steed, also operated two other Gold Coast nightclubs, the Club Royal and the Maple Grove Club, where he sold illegal liquor and offered gambling for a few years. But Steed's luck ran out on February 7, 1939, when Jackson police arrested him on charges of carrying a concealed weapon and vagrancy. Steed's arrest came just days after national guardsmen had raided all three of his nightclubs and destroyed gambling equipment. Biloxi's *Daily Herald* reported on February 8, 1939, that "Steed was carrying around $7,000 cash on his person and carried a large pistol" at the time he was arrested in Jackson. The news account continued by stating that Steed's "arrest was believed to be the first move in a campaign to prevent persons operating Rankin nightspots from finding refuge in Jackson. Mayor Walter A. Scott is believed cooperating with national guardsmen in a campaign to drive gold coast operators out of the Hinds-Rankin section." The article also mentioned Steed's earlier criminal record, stating that he "was sentenced in 1923 to a term of four years and fined $2,000 on a charge of violating the narcotic act. He was paroled, the record shows, in 1925. The state law provides persons shown not operating a business recognized as legal may be tried for vagrancy, police said." The exact timeframe during which Steed left the Hinds-Rankin County area after his trouble with local law enforcement is unclear, but some accounts indicate he may have become affiliated with another club in Desoto County, near the Mississippi-Tennessee state line, a known hot spot for illegal liquor and gambling. Research for this book, however, revealed that Doc Steed later may have left Mississippi entirely and settled near Bossier City, Louisiana, where the political climate was better suited for liquor and gambling. Interestingly, a road near Minden, Louisiana, east of Bossier City, now bears the name "Doc Steed Road."

Among the many other proprietors of Gold Coast nightclubs selling illegal liquor during the early years were Ernest Rogers, who ran the Oaks; Joe Catchings, proprietor of the Rocket Lounge; and Wayne Queen. An article in *American Mercury* magazine stated that Wayne Queen may have lasted in the Gold Coast area barely a year before he was convicted of grand larceny in Tunica County, north of Clarksdale, Mississippi. Although Queen was sentenced to serve a five-year term at Parchman Prison Farm, he served less than one year before he was paroled. Apparently Queen's status as an ex-con posed no problem for re-employment, as he was soon hired on as a deputy sheriff in Desoto County, Mississippi, where he moonlighted as a nightclub bouncer in his off-duty hours. In 1939, Queen's luck ran out when he was arrested in Memphis during a high-speed car chase, an incident that caused Governor White to revoke his parole and to order the ex-con back to Parchman Prison Farm. While Queen was out on bail, one of his former associates on the Gold Coast helped him hide out from the law. When someone finally informed Governor White that Queen had disappeared, he ordered state investigators to search for the former convict and return him to the state prison in Sunflower County.

"Hooch and Homicide in Mississippi"

By the late 1930s, the Gold Coast had emerged as a popular and vigorous nightclub scene, and many of the clubs stayed open twenty-four hours a day, seven days a week. Places like the Off-Beat Room at the Stamps Hotel, the Blue Flame, the Travelers Home and numerous other establishments featured entertainment by nationally known musicians. Among the better-known entertainers who performed at some of these clubs were Duke Ellington, Cab Calloway, Lena Horn and Billie Holiday, along with later blues legends Elmore James, Sonny Boy Williamson and a young entertainer from Itta Bena, Mississippi, named B.B. King. The Stamps Brothers Hotel, built about 1937 and operated by Charlie, Clift and Bill Stamps, was known throughout the South as an establishment that catered specifically to black patrons. The hotel's restaurant and club were tremendously popular with blacks who lived across the river in Jackson, and the owners brought in even more patrons with advertisements they ran in the *Jackson Advocate* that offered free bus service from Farish and Hamilton Streets to the Rankin County location. The restaurant at the Stamps Hotel offered a fine dining experience and served alcohol to its guests, but the hotel's Rankin Auditorium, with its five hundred seats and an enormous dance floor that could accommodate several thousand people, was the big draw. Often the site of live music performances

ANNOUNCEMENT

The Stamp Bros. Will Open Their New
Dining Room, Sunday, July 2nd, 1944

The New Dining Room will be called the

"Off Beat" Room

When you see it you'll agree that you can't beat the
"OFF BEAT" ROOM . . . . The South's Finest, with
its blanket of mirrors from front to back . . . . A real
treat for people who care, with connecting Private
Dining Rooms for Special Parties.

Dining -- Refreshments -- Music

Every Room in the Hotel Now Exclusively Private

For Information Dial 4-9278

THE STAMP

BROTHERS HOTEL

Fannin Road   East Jackson

Jackson Advocate, 1940's

An advertisement announcing a Gold Coast–
area hotel's new dining room. *Courtesy of Jackson
Advocate Archives.*

by big-name bands and nationally recognized performers, the Rankin County venue attracted both black and white clientele.

Craddock Goins wrote an article entitled "Hooch and Homicide in Mississippi" that appeared in the October 1939 edition of H.L. Mencken's magazine, *American Mercury*. Primarily, the article was an exposé of illegal liquor sales in a state with its own prohibition law and of the criminal activities that followed the sale of liquor. The article stated that L.G. Folse, executive director of the Mississippi State Planning Commission, "a fire-eating, hard-fisted, straight-talking, French-descent immigrant from Louisiana…issued a report bluntly describing bone-dry, Bible-belt Mississippi as the world's Number One crime center":

There is no place in the world where homicides are more prevalent than in Mississippi. In 1935 the homicide rate in Mississippi was higher than the homicide rate in any other country in the world, be it classed as civilized or uncivilized, religious or pagan, Christian or heathen…In 1935, there were 515 homicides in Mississippi, with the homicide rate of 26.2 for 100,000 population.

One of the first recorded mentions of Rankin County's Gold Coast may have been in the article by Goins, when he mentioned that "Jackson's Barbary Coast" was "known locally as the Gold Coast." Although Goins ridiculed the name Gold Coast, writing, "There is no coast except the hogwallows of the river banks," he gave credence to the name Barbary Coast when he added, "Plenty of gold crosses those banks to the pockets of the most brazen clique of cutthroats and bootleggers that ever defied the law." Later in the same article, Goins provided readers a comprehensive description of Rankin County, a place that many Hinds County residents continued to call "Sin City." The half-mile coast was dotted with shacks "costing $50 housing a $1500 bar and lavish gambling equipment over which Mississippians passed as much as $50,000 a week, according to estimates of the Jackson Chamber of Commerce," while the owners of the establishments claimed earning as much in a single weekend.

The cream of Mississippi society spends many a witch's Sabbath there, along with salaried men, wage hands, working girls, and plowboys. Strumpets and debutantes stand shoulder to shoulder at the crap tables and roulette wheels. Law-enforcement officials frequently are there in crap-shooting companionship with jailbirds. Negroes are segregated, but often a plantation landlord shoots dice with only a thin pine board between him and his cotton-pickers. It is nothing unusual for a police-court judge to swig liquor and gamble on the Coast one night and in court the next morning fine drunks who swigged at the same bar with him. Some of the state's most prominent citizens have mortgaged homes to follow the galloping dominoes and spinning wheels of the outlaw city. Housewives have dropped the family's grocery money…Public officials from all over the state have gathered to argue about temperance, politics, and drawing to inside straights.

Axes and Bayonets on the Gold Coast

As a result of Mencken's article in *American Mercury* and other allegations that whites and blacks in Rankin County openly enjoyed dining, drinking and dancing under the same roof, hundreds of enraged Mississippi citizens opposed to integrated activities in any form or fashion appealed to Governor White for help in shutting down these establishments. Governor White soon responded to public pressure from these individuals, his supporters and some Mississippi lawmakers and subsequently ordered another raid by 147 national guardsmen on Gold Coast establishments.

The *Biloxi Daily Herald* published a front-page article on June 23, 1939, reporting the results of the large-scale raid executed the night before on thirty-one Rankin County nightspots. During the raid, guardsmen wielding axes "destroyed 398 cases of liquor, 29 gaming tables, 9 first class bars and confiscated 84 slot machines, 21 electrical music boxes, and 12 guns." As a result of the raid, forty-one persons were arrested on various illegal liquor and gambling charges. A new state law making operation of a slot machine a penitentiary offense allowed the National Guard to padlock establishments where illegal liquor and gambling equipment were found. Major Birdsong, trouble shooter for Governor White and chief of the recent Rankin County raiding party, met with the governor about Gold Coast illegal activities and the fact that clubs "had always mushroomed back after the raiders sheathed their hatchets." Governor White "hinted martial law might be instituted." *The Delta Democrat-Times* reported that troopers armed with "axes and bayonets" confiscated liquor and gambling equipment valued at $50,670, making it the largest raid in "Gold Coast history."

A short time later, a political furor of sorts began when two Rankin County business owners, Dick Farr and R.B. Gressitt, filed charges in U.S. District Court against the Mississippi National Guard for illegal destruction of property, specifically gambling equipment, during the Rankin County raid. Biloxi's *Daily Herald* reported details of the pending lawsuit in its March 16, 1939 edition, stating that District Judge Sidney Carr Mize, recently appointed by President Franklin Roosevelt to the bench in the southern district of Mississippi, would decide the case. Research efforts to locate Judge Mize's decision, however, proved unsuccessful

In January 1940, shortly after he was elected Mississippi's forty-sixth governor, Paul Burney Johnson publicly advised his state's bootleggers to "close up" and "get out." A syndicated news article reported the announcement and stated the governor had two enforcement plans on his desk for consideration. One plan provided for a "home guard similar in most ways to the National Guard," and the other was called the Brady Plan, named for Colonel Thomas P. Brady, the state safety commissioner and commander of the Mississippi Highway Patrol. The Brady Plan proposed using state highway patrolmen to carry out the governor's orders to close up illegal liquor and gambling operations. Colonel Brady publicly stated he believed the already-trained Mississippi Highway Patrol group would be "almost as effective" as the National Guard during a "smash-up raid." Governor Johnson, however, had made no decision to use one plan or the other at the time the announcement was made. An explanation of the proposed Brady Plan appeared in the February 3, 1941 edition of Biloxi's *Daily News*, stating that "strict surveillance of all trucks going to and from all wholesale liquor establishments and strict enforcement of the many highway safety statutes" would be required. Some critics already had voiced opinions that raids would "prove much quicker and much more efficient" than "following every liquor truck to the state line for which it [was] officially destined" and "checking drivers for licenses, the weight of their loads, and other official requirements."

On February 22, 1941, the Biloxi newspaper reported the federal government had increased the strength of the Mississippi National Guard and announced, "The War Department came through to give the governor state troopers for…liquor raids and gambling cleanups." An executive order approved a regiment of 910 men for the Mississippi National Guard "for training and service" and for the time being would be at the governor's disposal for "liquor and gambling cleanups," although "technically, the unit would be under War Department orders if a national emergency warranted."

The Jeep, the Shady Rest and the Blue Flame

Among the dozens of liquor and gambling establishments eventually reopening on the Gold Coast after the raids in 1937 and 1939 were two nightclubs belonging to early Gold Coast operator Sam Seaney. Along with the Jeep Tourist Court, the local motor court he operated, Seaney owned two well-trafficked nightclubs, the Blue Flame (also known as the Spot) and the Shady Rest, a restaurant and bar. At the Jeep, Seaney allegedly rented rooms and sold liquor from the back of the building; customers drove up to a rear window or door and paid an attendant for liquor. The sale was finalized when the attendant passed a brown paper sack with the liquor inside back to the customer. Drive-around liquor sales, similar to Seaney's operation, continued on the Gold Coast for another two decades. Even my father, who admitted that he and some of his friends infrequently purchased liquor in Rankin County during the '50s and the '60s, remembered the gridlock of cars lined up around these drive-around Gold Coast liquor establishments on weekends. His description of the traffic into and out of these liquor businesses seemed reminiscent of a modern-day fast-food drive-through, where customers pull up in their cars and wait to buy burgers, fries and shakes instead of their favorite brand of whiskey.

One man who grew up in the Gold Coast area recalled that the Shady Rest contained a bar and an upscale restaurant downstairs. He described the building's unusual design around a large tree that grew up through the roof, recalling that the entire kitchen was designed to accommodate the bottom portion of the tree. An Italian chef from New Orleans prepared meals for guests in the lavish restaurant downstairs, and bartenders served liquor from the well-stocked bar. Upstairs, live music and after-dinner dancing were available for guests. By most accounts, the club saw a steady stream of patrons, many of them prominent and prosperous residents of Jackson and, on occasion, a few state lawmakers.

THE LIQUOR MAN AND THE LAWMAN

By 1940, the Gold Coast was known far and wide as *the* place to go to drink, dance and have a good time, and as its popularity increased, its nightclubs drew in big-name entertainers and huge crowds. But as the crowds rolled in and huge volumes of illegal liquor were consumed, the Gold Coast became a concentrated and thriving area of criminal activities. Routinely, liquor-fueled fights broke out, gunshots were fired and sometimes lives ended outside in the makeshift muddy parking lots near the clubs.

On January 30, 1940, *The Delta Democrat-Times* reported that newly elected Rankin County sheriff Graydon Holifield and his chief deputy, John Watts, along with several deputized citizens, had conducted "a succession of raids along Rankin's famed Gold Coast," where they confiscated twenty cases of liquor. Establishments raided included the Spot, the Pines, the Owl's Nest and the "black" Gold Coast. At the Spot, the sheriff and his deputies arrested Bob Jones and Roy Peacock for violating liquor laws. The two men appeared the following Friday before a local justice of the peace, where Jones was fined $100 and Peacock paid a $200 fine. Almost a month later, the Greenville newspaper reported Sheriff Holifield and his deputies had conducted two additional raids and confiscated ten cases of liquor on Saturday night of the previous weekend. On the day after the raid, Sheriff Holifield announced he and his staff planned to publicly destroy all confiscated liquor the next week during "a breaking-up party on the courthouse square." Apparently, the "breaking-up event" was a repeat of an earlier one held in the recent past and served as visible proof to the sheriff's supporters that he took his job seriously.

By virtue of his office and the oath he had taken when elected, the Rankin County sheriff was entrusted with full responsibility for enforcing the state's liquor laws in his county. During the 1940s, four individuals served as Rankin County's chief law enforcement officer. In 1942, H.P. Taylor succeeded

Graydon Holifield and served until 1944. H.G. Laird was elected to the office in 1944 and served until 1948, when Troy Mashburn replaced him until 1952. Throughout the 1940s and 1950s, the Gold Coast continued to grow, and the establishments there brought in tremendous amounts of revenue, much of it from illegal liquor sales. All indications were that Rankin County law enforcement prospered as well. One rumor circulated around the county in the 1940s alleging the sheriff took in more money than the highest-paid official in the United States. The same rumor also stated the source of most of the sheriff's income was from so-called protection money. The rumor indeed may have been true, since Rankin County, in 1946, paid the highest black market tax in the entire state.

The risk that came with serving as a member of law enforcement in Rankin County, however, was a tremendous one, something that became evident to the public on the night of August 19, 1946, when two men died in a gun battle at a Gold Coast establishment. Allegedly, Sam Seaney and Constable Norris Overby met at the Shady Rest, and after what some observers say was a very brief exchange of words, the two Rankin County men shot and killed each other. The August 19 edition of the *St. Petersburg (FL) Times* reported details of the shooting deaths, stating that Rankin County sheriff H.G. Laird said "the two men met in the doorway of Seaney's dance establishment crowded with 400 patrons, scuffled, drew guns, fired, and fell wounded… From their positions on the floor…they continued the duel, [with Seaney shooting Overby] through the chest" and Overby putting a bullet "through Seaney's body near the heart." One of Constable Overby's brothers, Ruell Overby, believed the raid on another nightclub may have caused the shooting. Shootings on the Gold Coast were not uncommon, and bodies often were found in the Pearl River. But this shooting was somehow different. In the days after the shooting, a public outcry went up like no other, and law enforcement and citizens alike knew that nothing short of shutting down the Gold Coast's illegal businesses would solve the liquor problem. In Biloxi, the aftermath of the Wild West–type duel between the liquor dealer and the lawman was the subject of a lengthy newspaper article appearing in the August 19 edition of Biloxi's *Daily Herald*. District Attorney A.B. McCraw of Philadelphia promised to investigate "liquor dealing, slot machines, and other law violations" when the Rankin County grand jury convened the following Monday. Circuit court judge Percy M. Lee, scheduled to preside over the grand jury in Brandon, promised to "have the situation on the Gold Coast stamped out…I am ready to help them close it up…and ready to help file any legal proceedings the people of Rankin County want filed."

Remembering the Gun Battle

Allen Peacock, now eighty years old and a Texas resident, grew up in Rankin County barely one hundred yards away from the Shady Rest, where the so-called duel occurred between Sam Seaney and Constable Norris Overby. Peacock recalled that his uncle Travis Tharp, his mother's brother, was tending bar at one of Seaney's nightclubs, the Spot, on the night of the gunfight. Constable Overby, he said, "strolled into the club, picked up a bottle of liquor, and walked out the door without paying for it." The constable rarely paid for liquor, since he was "on the sheriff's payroll." Peacock's uncle called Seaney, his boss, as soon as Overby left the Spot and reported that Overby had taken a bottle of liquor and did not pay for it. When the phone call was made, Seaney was at the Shady Rest, which he also owned, and where Peacock's father worked as a bartender. Peacock explained that his father told him soon after the shooting that Overby arrived at the Shady Rest just minutes after he left the Spot, as the two clubs were quite close. Peacock's father told him that Overby entered the Shady Rest through the front door and walked past the bar area where he worked, and with the purloined bottle of liquor in hand, he proceeded to the red-carpeted, mirrored hallway that led four steps up to the club's dance hall. As Overby attempted to enter the dance hall, Seaney appeared in the doorway, and for a moment, the two men looked at each other, facing off "eyeball to eyeball." Peacock added that Overby "tried to walk past Seaney to go into the dance hall." In that brief moment, Peacock said, the two men quickly exchanged words, and gunshots were fired. The elder Peacock watched as Overby fell on the floor at the top of the stairs. Seaney fell down the stairs and ended up on the carpeted hallway floor below. Although the two men were down, they were still within each other's sight, and as they lay in their respective spots, the liquor dealer and the constable exchanged shots once again, finally killing each other.

Some of the older individuals interviewed during research for this book still believe the shooting at the Shady Rest nightclub was the impetus for law enforcement's shutdown of many nightclubs and liquor joints along the Gold Coast. In hindsight, the incident may have been the end of what some called the glory days in Rankin County. The *St. Petersburg (FL) Times* ran a follow-up article on September 4, 1946, barely two weeks after the shooting incident, reporting Rankin County's immediate plans for legal action. After a grand jury was impaneled, Circuit Judge Percy M. Lee called on the panel of jurors "composed primarily of farmers" to investigate Gold Coast activities "highlighted by a gun battle last week." Joe Sanderson, a local farmer and sawmill operator, headed the group of jurors. District Attorney A.B. McCraw conferred with the jurymen and later announced plans to "call on the state to help him in his drive against liquor selling and gambling on the glittering gold coast," since Lieutenant Governor Fielding Wright, acting in Governor Bailey's absence, said he had received no request for help from the state guard.

G.W. "Big Red" Hydrick

One of the more memorable mid-century Gold Coast liquor dealers was George Washington "G.W." Hydrick, a red-haired, ruddy-faced man better known as "Big Red." Hydrick, born in Simpson County on February 11, 1906, was nicknamed Red by his parents because of his hair color. The word "Big" was added to his name in later years to differentiate between Hydrick and his younger brother, Xavier L. Hydrick, who was known as "Little Red" to his family and friends. Big Red Hydrick, raised on a farm, grew up in a large family that worked hard to survive the Great Depression years. Like other young men of that time, Big Red married young, and he and his wife, Lottie Becknell Hydrick, soon became parents of five children: James, Benjamin Cary, Loyd, Willie Mae and Jack Kenneth. As his family grew, Hydrick increasingly found it difficult to provide adequately for them. The U.S. Census recorded in 1940 for Rankin County listed Hydrick's occupation as a service station attendant. Later, Hydrick worked as a night watchman at a liquor warehouse in the up-and-coming Gold Coast area of Rankin County. As Hydrick kept watch over a warehouse of liquor, he paid particular attention to the expensive clothes and fancy cars flaunted by some Gold Coast bootleggers. Willie Mae (Hydrick) Bradshaw, in *Red*, the biography she wrote about her father, said Hydrick decided he could earn more money if he became a bootlegger like the well-heeled men he saw on the Gold Coast. Hydrick had a huge problem, however. He had no money to buy even a few bottles of liquor to resell.

Bradshaw recalled that her father's venture into the liquor business began when he decided to ask a friend, a local Rankin County banker, for a fifty-dollar bank loan. Mustering up the courage to talk to the banker was troublesome for Hydrick, his daughter wrote, since a stutter he developed in childhood made it difficult for him to communicate clearly. But Hydrick proceeded with his plan to meet with the banker and request a loan. Although the banker denied Hydrick's request, he felt sorry for the man with a stutter who barely had a dollar in his pocket and decided to lend Hydrick fifty dollars of his own money. Pleasantly surprised by his good fortune, Hydrick thanked the friend for his generosity and promised to repay the money as soon as he could. One bit of information, however, was missing from Hydrick's interaction with the Rankin County banker that day; he failed to tell his friend that he intended to buy illegal liquor with the money so that he could become a liquor dealer. Allegedly, Hydrick fulfilled his promise and repaid the debt to his banker friend within a few months. Her father's liquor business, Bradshaw wrote, began along a well-traveled Rankin County highway, where Hydrick set up a small liquor stand near the roadway and sold bottles of booze from the trunk of his car. One Jackson-area man wrote an article, published in 2004 in the *Mississippi Business Journal*, about a highway intersection near the location where Red Hydrick first sold liquor:

> *The intersection of Highway 80 and Highway 51 (Terry Road) was a major crossroads before the Interstate system came along. Highway 80 stretches 2,726 miles east and west from Savannah, Ga., to San Diego, Calif., while Highway 51 runs north and south from Chicago to New Orleans…Men stood on the median and sold peanuts and newspapers to motorists waiting for the traffic light to change. Everyone knew that gangster Red Hydrick lived at the Alamo Plaza Motel, which was located on the southeast side of the intersection.*

As Hydrick continued to buy and sell liquor, his profits increased, and he soon moved over to the fast-growing Rankin County area known as the Gold Coast, where he made a name for himself as a large-volume liquor dealer. In the years that followed, some who knew Red Hydrick well recalled that he became a very wealthy bootlegger. His daughter confirmed that information in her father's biography, stating that he provided his family with a large, comfortable home and pampered his children with lavish gifts that ranged from horses to expensive jewelry.

After the Gold Coast gun battle in 1946, public sentiment and, more likely, political embarrassment fueled events that eventually brought serious changes to the way Hydrick and other liquor dealers operated. One of the most significant of these events was the Rankin County grand jury investigation immediately following the shootout. An Associated Press article in the September 8, 1946 edition of *The Delta Democrat-Times* discussed the potential effects of the grand jury investigation, saying that "a total and permanent closure of Rankin County's gold coast" would result in a tremendous loss of revenue for the state of Mississippi. Tax figures included in the article showed that Rankin County was one of the state's "leading sources of revenue from the black market tax on illegal liquor sales." The article continued, stating records obtained from the office of the state tax collector, Carl Craig, showed that "Rankin County liquor dealers had paid black market tax during the first eight months of calendar year 1946 in these amounts: January, $86,111; February, $90,610; March, $139,460; April, $114,106; May, $120,429; June, $82,233; and July, approximately $100,000." The news account also identified three additional Mississippi counties—Sunflower (Indianola), Warren (Vicksburg) and Harrison (Biloxi and Gulfport)—that had paid black market taxes averaging more than $10,000 each per month.

A separate article in the same edition of the newspaper reported that Rankin County district attorney A.B. McCraw had announced the names of four individuals indicted after the recent grand jury probe: Mr. and Mrs. G.W. Hydrick and their two adult sons, James and T. Hydrick. The attorney representing the four Hydrick family members promised to "attack the legality of the search warrant used in making the seizure of approximately 800 cases of liquor which McCraw has estimated to be worth $100,000." Three days later, the newspaper reported the Rankin County Grand Jury found it "utterly impossible to get positive information" on liquor-law violations in the county's wide-open Gold Coast area. Although the grand jury reported it had "examined 100 witnesses and returned 21 indictments," only four of the indictments returned were against Gold Coast operators. The grand jury's announcement also included a recommendation that "Mississippi residents play a part in bringing liquor law violations to light in the notorious district, and that peace officers make a 'special and determined effort' to eliminate the possession and sale of liquor and to stamp out operation of Gold Coast honky-tonks."

In the weeks and months following the indictments, however, illegal activities along the Gold Coast did not stop, and Rankin County citizens complained that little had changed after the grand jury investigation. Instead of requesting National Guard enforcement assistance from Governor Fielding Wright, Rankin County sheriff H.G. Laird ordered county deputies and other local law enforcement officers to conduct raids on Gold Coast liquor and gambling operations. On May 23, 1947, *The Delta Democrat-Times* reported that Sheriff Laird and his deputies had conducted "raids netting

125 cases of liquor during the past 10 days [and] have 'blackened out' the glittering 'Gold Coast' area." Sheriff Laird issued the statement after his "recent meetings with Rankin County citizens who protested liquor and gambling in the 'Gold Coast' area which catered to patrons in Jackson." The sheriff estimated the liquor seized was valued at $7,000 and admitted publicly that "large caches of liquor had been moved from the county." Sheriff Laird added that his deputies were still searching for the hidden liquor. Although Sheriff Laird repeatedly said he and his deputies had the Gold Coast situation under control, the local citizens' group believed Rankin County establishments were still selling liquor.

Hydrick's daughter wrote that local law enforcement had warned a few of the better-connected liquor dealers, including her father, that raids were imminent, allowing them to move their inventories into hiding until things cooled off. She explained that Hydrick moved his liquor inventory from the building where he stored it on the Gold Coast to a large hay barn located on her family's farm near Florence, Mississippi. Soon after the sheriff and his deputies raided Gold Coast liquor and gambling operations in May 1947, deputies also raided Hydrick's Florence farm, where they discovered nearly eight hundred cases of liquor carefully concealed with hay. Bradshaw wrote about the raid at her family's farm and described the chaotic scene that existed as the large liquor supply was seized. When she got off the school bus that day, armed Rankin County officers and their vehicles were on the premises. Neither Hydrick nor her mother was at home when the officers arrived, but Bradshaw said her mother returned soon after the raid began. Although Bradshaw was a young girl at the time of the incident, she remembered the event well and described the events unfolding as she watched the men remove cases of liquor from the hay barn and load them onto a large truck. After the raid was over, an observer, possibly a reporter for one of the local newspapers, snapped a photo of a flatbed truck loaded with cases and loose bottles of confiscated liquor just before the officers prepared to drive away. In the photo, a Rankin County officer named L.G. Holifield stood near the cargo of seized liquor. Several decades later, the deputy's family donated certain Holifield family memorabilia, including the photo of the truckload of liquor, to the Brandon Public Library in Rankin County. Attempts to obtain a copy of that photo for this book, however, were unsuccessful.

Hydrick's daughter believed the primary event that shaped the future of her father's liquor business began with the warning he received from local law enforcement about the Gold Coast raid. He felt as if he had been betrayed by law enforcement, since only someone in authority in Rankin

County knew where he had hidden his liquor supply. Soon after Hydrick's liquor was hauled away from the barn, allegedly headed for destruction, the Rankin County sheriff allowed some of the county's liquor dealers to return to their former Gold Coast establishments. Bradshaw wrote that Hydrick, however, was not among the dealers officially invited to return. Eventually, she said, Hydrick did reestablish his Rankin County liquor business with thirty-five cases of liquor authorities failed to discover during the raid at his Florence farm.

In mid-century Mississippi, Big Red Hydrick was known by dealers and customers alike as a big-time, well-connected bootlegger. But among members of the black community in Hinds County, Hydrick was considered a racist. Over the bridge in Jackson, Hydrick often told anyone who would listen that he had been "deputized" by the Jackson police chief, and he frequently flashed a shiny badge to prove his alleged "honorary officer" status. Hydrick's belief that he was a real-life part of Hinds County law enforcement may have been the reason he was present outside Jackson's city courts building in late March 1961 when approximately one hundred Negroes gathered in support of nine college students charged with breach of peace for staging a sit-in demonstration earlier that month at Jackson's all-white public library. An Associated Press article in the March 30, 1961 edition of the *Indiana* (PA) *Gazette*, just weeks before the sit-in incident, reported that "G.W. (Red) Hydrick, 55, a Rankin County white bootlegger, was charged with assault and battery and carrying a concealed weapon after he pistol-whipped Thomas Armstrong...a Negro who writes for a Jackson newspaper and does freelance photography." Local law enforcement arrested Hydrick and confiscated his gun, but he soon posted bond. Later, when Hydrick appeared in court, he was required to pay a $125 fine, and his gun was returned.

Two months later, on May 28, 1961, Hydrick was present at the well-documented sit-in demonstration held at Woolworth's lunch counter in downtown Jackson. A syndicated photograph of the sit-in, taken by Jackson photographer Fred Blackwell, pictured Hydrick standing behind a group of onlookers and hecklers at the lunch counter just before the student activists were arrested by Jackson police officers. The following August, Hydrick was arrested and charged with injuring a man at a local Jackson drive-in restaurant. On August 22, 1961, *The Delta Democrat-Times* reported that "G.W. (Big Red) Hydrick, a convicted bootlegger [was] free under a $2,000 bond...on charges of shooting and wounding a Jackson man at a drive-in Sunday morning." William E. Puckett, the injured man, was reported in "fair condition" at Baptist Hospital. Hydrick shot the man "near the mouth

An aerial photo of Jackson, 1950s. *Courtesy of Mississippi Department of Archives and History.*

during a scuffle…Hydrick said he intended to hit Puckett with the pistol, but it discharged accidentally." Eight people witnessed the shooting and said the incident stemmed from Puckett's accusation of Hydrick "cutting some telephone wires." Hydrick was tried in Hinds County Circuit Court for assault and battery with intent to kill, and he was convicted of the charge by a jury. Presiding Judge Leon Hendrick fined the fifty-five-year-old bootlegger $1,000 and sentenced him to serve one year in the county penitentiary. Hydrick's attorneys stated they planned to file an appeal with the Mississippi Supreme Court, and Hydrick remained free on a $2,000 appeal bond. Research for this book found no evidence of a subsequent appeal or a record of state prison time served.

Hydrick's daughter wrote that her father received no protection from local law enforcement in the years after he reestablished his illegal liquor business on the banks of the Pearl River. Instead, he and a few men who worked for him spent numerous hours devising various ways to ensure that alcohol agents and the local sheriff's office could neither locate nor seize his liquor inventory ever again. Among the methods, tricks and devices used were a high wall he built to conceal his property, a hidden room with a false wall where he hid liquor inside the building and a pulley system that Hydrick and his helpers devised to retrieve bottles of booze hidden in the overgrowth along the Pearl River that ran beside his place. Hydrick lived in the small building where he hid his liquor supply, and his daughter recalled that he slept with a gun beside him. As extra security, one of Hydrick's longtime employees, an elderly black man, kept watch in a small building nearby. Although Hydrick's liquor sales continued, his last years in business were unlike the glitzy years on the Gold Coast he remembered from years past. The days when he was known as a big-time bootlegger with political clout, law enforcement connections and an expensive antique car collection were forever behind him. And in June 1966, with a local option law in place and an effective date just around the corner, Hydrick knew his only option was to shut down the illegal liquor business he had operated for almost twenty-seven years.

Pearl River below Low Head Dam, pictured at low-water stage on November 8, 1963. *Courtesy of Mississippi Department of Archives and History.*

Red Hydrick lived for almost eight more years before he died in a tragic accident that happened near the place where he had sold liquor for several decades. His daughter wrote that Hydrick died on September 11, 1974, and details of his death were based on an eyewitness account of the neighbor and friend who last saw him alive. The woman explained that Hydrick had dropped off several baby ducks she had asked him to bring by her home that morning. He attempted to place the ducklings inside the woman's fenced yard, but she told him she was afraid the small creatures might be eaten by some animals that had been in her yard the night before. At that point, she asked Hydrick to place the ducklings in the river nearby where they would be more protected. Hydrick did as the woman requested and subsequently made several trips up and down the steep, muddy banks of the Pearl River until he had placed all the ducklings in the water. On his final climb up the treacherous bank, the woman recalled, Hydrick slipped and fell backward into the river below, where he was quickly swept away by the current. In a sad but ironic twist of fate, the Pearl River that Hydrick once used to hide his liquor supply also concealed his body for three days before it was discovered downstream.

XAVIER L. "LITTLE RED" HYDRICK

Allegedly, the life of Red Hydrick's youngest brother, Xavier L. Hydrick, ended in a river over two decades earlier. The *Brandon News* reported on February 15, 1951, that X.L. Hydrick, commonly known as "Little Red," disappeared on February 8 during a trip across the Yazoo Canal near Vicksburg. His death or whereabouts were still unknown six days after the incident. S.C. Moncure, manager of the *Showboat* nightclub, reported to officers that X.L. Hydrick had been on board the gambling boat "between early Wednesday night and closing time on Thursday morning" and that Hydrick had attempted "to hold him up for the *Showboat*'s receipts for the day" as they were returning to Vicksburg on a small ferryboat. Moncure said the incident happened about 2:30 in the morning and admitted that he hit Hydrick with his fist and "knocked him off" the ferryboat into the waters of the Yazoo Canal. Moncure added that the last time he saw Hydrick, he was "swimming toward the Louisiana bank, just below the *Showboat*." Later, Moncure told Vicksburg police and Sheriff Hester that he did not have the day's receipts with him when the incident occurred and that he had sent the money earlier to Vicksburg with a friend. Haley E. Dye, Hydrick's friend who had driven him to Vicksburg, told authorities that Hydrick was unarmed. Officers searched the Louisiana side of the canal but failed to find Hydrick, and Sheriff Hester publicly stated that he believed Hydrick swam safely to shore. Vicksburg chief of police Albert Allen contended that Hydrick likely drowned, while unverified rumors surfaced that Hydrick had been seen on Thursday after the altercation. Historical newspaper articles document that Hydrick's badly decomposed body was found about three months later by Herman Lynn, a fisherman, near Palmyra Island, approximately eighteen miles south of Vicksburg. Although it seems probable that X.L. Hydrick was involved in his older brother's illegal liquor business, documentation of that relationship was not found during research for this book.

X.L. Hydrick's son, Ken Hydrick Flessas, said his father had several children by at least three women, but he never married all the women. His mother was Doris Sewell of Pensacola, Florida, whose marriage to X.L. Hydrick lasted from 1938 to 1943, when the couple divorced. At birth, Flessas was named Henry Kendral Hydrick, but his name was changed when he was adopted at a young age by his stepfather. Although Flessas spent most of his young years growing up in another state, he did remember visiting his father; his uncle, Red Hydrick; and other relatives who worked on the Gold Coast. Flessas recalled that Rankin County liquor dealers had "little shacks, and traffic that came from Jackson (politicians, lawyers, judges, preachers, etc.) drove by and reached out to take that little brown bag and pass money back."

A Local Man Remembers the Gold Coast

One individual who remembered life along the Gold Coast was Davie Ricardo Lindsey, the son of club owner and bartender Jimmy Lindsey. Davie Lindsey stated that his father owned and operated a nightclub called the Gay Lady, where he also worked as a bartender. Lindsey and his family lived five doors down from the club and just around the corner from the Blue Flame, another nightclub managed by his father. The Blue Flame, Lindsey explained, was taken over by Gold Coast bootlegger Red Hydrick after the original owner, Sam Seaney, died in a shootout with the Brandon constable Norris Overby. As a young man growing up in a neighborhood of nightclubs where hundreds of patrons gathered seven nights a week, Lindsey remembers the all-too-frequent shootings and stabbings, as well as the raids by law enforcement. Crime and chaos aside, Lindsey added that he still has fond memories of the many jazz and blues musicians, especially Ella Fitzgerald, Ike and Tina Turner and Billie Holiday, who frequented the Gay Lady nightclub. With a father who owned one nightclub and managed another, ten-year-old Lindsey and his younger brother literally "picked up" some spending money when they helped clean the Gay Lady nightclub on Sunday mornings. Lindsey explained that the clubs were open until the wee hours of Sunday morning, and there was very little time to clean the place before it reopened for business. His responsibility, and that of his brother, was to "clean around the slot machines in the back room of the club." Lindsey believed the job was a pretty exciting one, since he and his brother usually found a couple of dollars in nickels and dimes around the slot machines. Lindsey laughingly remarked that a couple of dollars was "a lot of money back then, especially for young boys in the 1950s."

Lindsey recalled meeting Red Hydrick and said the man who paid his father to manage the Blue Flame was often in the company of his "light-skinned black lady friend, Miss Amy Atwood." Although Lindsey said he knew "Mr. Red" was married and had children, he also knew the older man spent most nights in the back of the club where his lady friend lived. As Lindsey grew into a teenager, he soon realized that many activities at Gold Coast clubs were against the law. Although he did not remember seeing "well-known white folks from Jackson" and other parts of Hinds County at the clubs, Lindsey said his father explained to him that "dignitaries and legislators entertained their girlfriends at the Airways Inn," a nearby motel, "not at places on the Gold Coast."

Toward the end of our conversation, Lindsey suggested that I contact an elderly woman he called "Mama Stamps," who was married to one of the three Stamps brothers and had managed the well-known Stamps Hotel for many years. Believing that Mama Stamps might be helpful in piecing together information about the Gold Coast's early years, Lindsey gave me her phone number. Unfortunately, the woman's nephew answered the phone and sadly reported that his aunt had passed away the previous week.

Chapter 10

The Mississippi Gulf Coast

The Mississippi Gulf Coast, with its proximity to Mobile, New Orleans and ports in the Caribbean, has a long history of involvement in the illegal liquor trade. Rumrunners from Cuba, Puerto Rico and elsewhere in the Caribbean often sought safe haven in the secluded bays and coves along the Gulf of Mexico beaches when they arrived in the coastal waters of the United States. Throughout the early part of the twentieth century, oceangoing ships of various types and sizes, laden with heavy loads of contraband liquor, frequently were seized by alcohol agents and other law enforcement officials. Very rarely was all the liquor confiscated, however, and on more than a few occasions, the illegal booze ended up in Biloxi and Gulfport, where Gulf Coast citizens frequently were at odds with liquor sales, gambling and prostitution and where public corruption seemed to thrive. When railroads were built in the region, the Gulf Coast became an inland shipping point for contraband liquor purchased from Caribbean distilleries. Numerous archived newspaper accounts reported that literally thousands of cases of liquor in the twentieth century arrived in vessels "docked discreetly in the secluded inlets along the coastline," and the cargoes were "consigned to railroad cars" as lumber shipments. Since the majority of the shipments were headed to Chicago and New York, federal authorities suspected the activities were connected to crime syndicates in the two cities. Many who observed the Gulf Coast's seemingly lawless activities over the years believed the two-hundred-mile

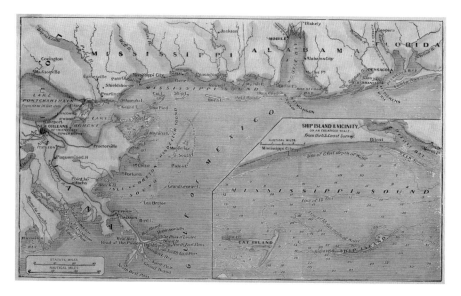

An early map of Mississippi's Gulf of Mexico coastline. *Courtesy of Mississippi Department of Archives and History.*

distance south of Jackson, the capital, allowed Gulf Coast businesses the opportunity to function almost independently of the state's liquor and gambling laws.

THE ISLE OF CAPRICE HOTEL AND RESORT

Dog Key Island, commonly referred to as simply "Dog Key," was among several barrier islands that once existed along the Mississippi Sound. Conveniently located twelve miles outside the jurisdiction of the United States and historically a popular location for local fishermen, Dog Key became a haven for bootleggers in the 1920s. The island was small, just three miles long and roughly five hundred acres in size, but Dog Key had precious artesian springs that provided fresh water to fisherman. Bootleggers also used the clean, clear water to make moonshine, which they transported from the island back to the mainland where it was sold. Three men, Colonel Jack W. Apperson, Walter "Skeet" Hunt and Arbeau Caillavet, believed that Dog Key's location made it an ideal location for a hotel and resort that offered liquor and gambling. Their idea became a reality, and the men named their

White House Hotel, Biloxi. *Courtesy of Mississippi Department of Archives and History.*

new business enterprise the Isle of Caprice Hotel and Resort. On July 5, 1925, the long-awaited resort opened its doors to the public. Transportation to the new resort was by boat, and four vessels—the *Silver Moon*, the *Jolly Jack*, the *Charles Redding* and the *Margaret*—were on hand to transport guests from designated landings at the Biloxi Yacht Club, Wachenfeld's Pier, the White House and the Riviera Pavillion.

The largest of the vessels was the *Silver Moon*, owned by Ed Moran, a fifty-five-foot pleasure boat capable of carrying 150 passengers. As passengers waited at the Riviera Pavillion to make the maiden voyage to Dog Key, the Buena Vista Orchestra entertained them with music. By most accounts, initial trips to the island took roughly thirty minutes, and a one-way fare cost less than one dollar. The Isle of Caprice was a huge success during its first year of business, and when the resort began its second season, the *Pan American* joined other vessels in transporting guests to the island. Captained by Peter Skrmetti, the converted sixty-six-foot schooner, capable of carrying about 200 passengers, made twice-daily trips from Desporte's Pier to the resort. One of the *Pan American*'s most unique features was a small platform on board that served as a dance floor. Later in 1926, Captain Earnest L. Moran began making trips to the Isle of Caprice in his charter boat, the *Iona Louise*, picking up passengers at the Biloxi Yacht Club and Buena Vista Hotel piers in early afternoon. At six

Isle of Caprice Hotel and Resort on Dog Island, twelve miles off the coast of Biloxi. *Courtesy of Mississippi Department of Archives and History.*

Buena Vista Pavilion as it appeared in the 1930s. *Courtesy of Mississippi Department of Archives and History.*

The entrance to Buena Vista Hotel, circa 1940. *Courtesy of Mississippi Department of Archives and History.*

Excursion boats on Biloxi Bay, 1930s. *Courtesy of Mississippi Department of Archives and History.*

o'clock each evening, Captain Moran began the voyage back to Biloxi, where he returned guests to their respective locations. During the same time period, Ed Moran, Captain Moran's brother, continued to provide transportation on the *Silver Moon*, and Captain Foster Swetman also made voyages back and forth in his craft, the *Water Witch*.

Since frequent and comfortable transportation to the island was vital to the resort's success, the owners ensured guests made future trips to the island in style. On January 19, 1928, Biloxi's *Daily Herald* reported that resort owners had charged Henry Brasher of Brasher Shipyard in North Biloxi with upgrading a former government and pilot boat to a larger and safer excursion boat. The refurbished excursion boat would feature rebuilt decks, a new pilot house and a "glass enclosed cabin and a dance floor." A unique feature of the glass-enclosed cabin area was the presence of "glass windows that could be raised and lowered, depending on the weather and the temperature." When guests arrived at the island resort, they could drink the best liquor available and wager their money against luck at slot machines, roulette wheels and dice games. The success of the Isle of Caprice, however, was short-lived. As history has proven throughout the years, and as survivors of Camille, Katrina and all the other past hurricanes that many Gulf Coast residents remember so well, the warm Gulf waters have a mind of their own. Soon, nature and the environment had their way with the small island with a history of erosion from storms and currents, and by 1932, Dog Key's jewel, the Isle of Caprice, was submerged by the waters of the Gulf of Mexico.

FINANCIERS, OPERATING DIRECTORS AND "THE STRIP"

As more and more bootleggers and liquor dealers flocked to the Gulf Coast, eager to start their own restaurants, hotels and nightclubs, crime syndicates began relocating their liquor and gambling establishments in Biloxi and Gulfport. An article in the *Times-Picayune*, the longtime New Orleans newspaper, reported these individuals were part of a "more or less undefined organization of financiers and operating directors." As illegal activities along the coast grew in number, crime also increased. After U.S. Prohibition ended, the United States government shifted its enforcement responsibility against illegal liquor dealers from the Justice Department to the U.S. Treasury Department, and the Mississippi Gulf Coast area was suddenly in the sights of federal revenue agents. Using resources newly available to them at the time, including wiretaps, federal agents seized numerous railroad cars of liquor allegedly destined for inland locations, including New York and Chicago, during the early years of enforcement activities. The U.S. Coast Guard's interdiction of several vessels with large caches of contraband liquor aboard was reported in the *Biloxi Daily Herald* on January 28, 1932. The news article identified the U.S. Coast Guard *301*, a patrol boat from the Biloxi base, as the vessel that seized the *Freda*, an auxiliary schooner owned by Bernard Taltavull of the Biloxi Canning Company, off Pass Christian in late January. The boat contained a cargo of contraband liquor valued at more than $60,000. Arrested were Captain Robert McDonald and Benny Frenefi of Pass Christian; Roy Sconyern of Hugo, Oklahoma; Albert Boudreaux, Martin Ross and James Freche of Biloxi; Henry Latimer of Gulfport; and Arthur Birou of New Orleans. The vessel had allegedly been on an oystering trip to the Pass Christian reefs. The U.S. Coast Guard also had captured the *Alena*, a rum lugger from New Orleans, with nine hundred cases of alcohol and liquor on board and had seized the *Blanche Marie* with 1,600 sacks of liquor.

Although several historic hotels dating back to the Gay Nineties already existed along the Gulf Coast, numerous others sprang up along U.S.

Edgewater Gulf Hotel at Biloxi, circa 1950. *Courtesy of Mississippi Department of Archives and History.*

Markham Hotel, Biloxi, circa 1940. *Courtesy of Mississippi Department of Archives and History.*

Tivoli Hotel, Biloxi. *Courtesy of Mississippi Department of Archives and History.*

Highway 90 (later Beach Boulevard) during the 1930s as the well-trafficked highway made its way through Louisiana and along the white beaches of the Mississippi Gulf Coast. The Broadwater Beach, the Edgewater Gulf, the Tivoli, the Markham Hotel and the White House were among some of the hotels built during that period. Each establishment offered luxurious accommodations, elegant dining and lounges and bars with an array of alcoholic beverages. As restaurants, nightclubs, gambling joints and small motor courts and guest houses were built along the east–west thoroughfare, tourism grew and flourished. Thousands of vacationers flocked to the area that many referred to as Mississippi's own Riviera, seeking its subtropical climate, pristine beaches and cool ocean breezes. After a day of fun in the sun, visitors could dine on fresh-caught seafood and visit local nightclubs, where they drank, gambled and danced until early morning. Although liquor and gambling were illegal, business owners and Gulf Coast visitors alike seemed oblivious to the fact, and when visitors left, it was with anticipation of a return trip to what became known as "The Strip."

"Clean Up or Be Closed Up"

Newly elected Harrison County sheriff R.C. Edwins was sworn into office on January 1, 1940. As the chief law enforcement officer of the county where Biloxi was located, the new sheriff vowed to rid his jurisdiction of illegal liquor, gambling and crime. By the end of May, Sheriff Edwins and his deputies had confiscated approximately 1,700 bottles of bonded whiskey and seized thirty-eight slot machines discovered during response calls to clubs where complaints of disorderly conduct had been made. On May 31, 1940, Biloxi's *Daily Herald* reported that Sheriff Edwins and his deputies had destroyed confiscated slot machines and liquor they had left for viewing in the yard of the county jail on the previous day. About $500 was also recovered from the slot machines and "deposited to the credit of the general county fund." On June 1, 1941, Sheriff Edwins and twelve deputies raided an unidentified East Howard Avenue business where they confiscated large quantities of bonded whiskey and high alcoholic volume wine and arrested one individual. During the same raid, the sheriff and his deputies observed gambling in progress and noted slot machines, dice tables, poker chips, money and other evidence of illegal gambling activity, although the news article did not mention the disposition of the gambling machines and paraphernalia. After months of raiding Harrison County's illegal liquor and gambling joints, Sheriff Edwins became dissatisfied with the results and issued a forty-eight-hour ultimatum to liquor and gambling establishments, ordering the business operators to "clean up or be closed up."

Two weeks later, Sheriff Edwins and his deputies raided a number of prominent Biloxi nightspots overnight on June 15–16. A dozen or more individuals were arrested on liquor charges and for maintaining illegal gambling operations, including M.N. Mickal (Union Bar); Grover Graham Sr., owner of two unnamed establishments; ex–deputy sheriff Jimmy Williams (Marietta Café); Shirod Miller (Buena Vista Hotel Cocktail Lounge); Gus Sullwold (Roof Bar); and Pete Nichols of the Broadwater Beach Hotel.

RELIGIOUS GROUPS, CITY OFFICIALS AND LAWMAKERS

Historical news articles indicate a small number of Biloxi citizens supported the local sheriff's efforts, and two adult Sunday school groups—the Susannah Bible Class and the Wesley Bible Class of the Gulfport First United Methodist Church—unanimously signed numbered documents on September 9, 1940, endorsing his actions. The public endorsements were signed by the male and female members of the two Sunday school classes, and several individuals signing the documents also made short speeches praising Sheriff Edwins for his dedication and efforts to rid the area of illegal liquor, gambling and related activities. Apparently the sheriff's efforts were not enough, and in 1943, the Biloxi Protestant Pastors Association, in response to local church members and other citizens opposed to liquor and gambling, endorsed a resolution they presented to Biloxi's mayor and city officials. The resolution's language was simple and to the point; it asked public officials to enforce illegal liquor and slot machine activity taking place within the city. But the group's appeal seemingly was in vain. Two other groups subsequently attempted to talk law enforcement into cracking down on illegal liquor businesses, but their efforts failed, as well.

News reports of raids conducted during the 1940s and items seized during the raids indicate that local law enforcement may have spent more time confiscating gambling equipment than enforcing the sale of illegal liquor. In fact, an atmosphere of "looking the other way" instead of taking enforcement action against liquor dealers seemed to prevail. Some residents believed that enforcement of illegal liquor temporarily had been curtailed, and rumors were rampant that talk of another local option bill to be introduced in the

Mississippi legislature was making the rounds. As history soon revealed, the state's political and religious factions continued with their reluctance to legalize liquor, and a local option bill was not voted on until 1952. During the same time period, the *Daily Herald* reported that Claude V. Bilbo, who represented Jackson County in the Mississippi legislature, had proposed the legalization of alcohol sales in Mississippi. Representative Bilbo explained the rationale behind his proposal was a very simple one; an estimated $3.2 million in tax revenues could be collected over the next two years, provided the law could be passed. But Bilbo's proposal fell on deaf ears, at least in the Gulf Coast region, and law enforcement officials continued with raids and the seizure of illegal liquor.

The attitude of another Mississippi lawmaker who represented the Gulf Coast during state prohibition was evident during a senate committee meeting in early March 1946. *The Delta Democrat-Times* reported on March 14, 1946, that State Senator Howard McDonnell of Biloxi, an "outspoken anti-prohibitionist," had spoken out the day before against a bill authored by Senator C.W. Sullivan. The bill was intended to "enable the federal government to aid the state in enforcing the anti-liquor laws." Senator Sullivan explained that his bill, patterned after a law already in effect in the state of Oklahoma, prevented liquor exceeding 4 percent alcohol content from import or transport into the state "without a permit from the secretary of state." During debate, Senator McDonnell spoke against the bill, stating it would "make sneaks out of honest men down my way." During later discussion, the senator spoke freely about liquor sales on the Gulf Coast when he explained, "The liquor business is a legitimate business where I come from, and the passage of this law won't do anything more than increase the price of liquor." The committee voted twenty-six to seventeen to report the bill favorably to the entire body, although by all accounts, the bill was never approved.

The Kefauver Crime Committee Hearings and Investigation

The website of the U.S. Senate details the history behind the May 3, 1950 establishment of the Kefauver Crime Committee, stating the committee was launched as a result of the "assassination of a gambling kingpin who was found in April 1950 in a Democratic clubhouse, slumped beneath a large portrait of President Harry S. Truman. His assassination intensified national concerns about the post–World War II growth of powerful crime syndicates and the resulting gang warfare in the nation's largest cities." The five-member Special Committee to Investigate Organized Crime in Interstate Commerce included members of the Interstate Commerce and Judiciary Committees, as well as each committee's senior Republican, and was chaired by Tennessee freshman senator Estes Kefauver.

During the time the Kefauver Crime Committee was convened, its members received alarming allegations that airmen stationed at Keesler Airfield in Biloxi were pawning their shoes and clothing and stealing money to pay gambling debts owed at various clubs located near the base. As a result of the allegations, a Senate Armed Services Committee held a hearing on October 22, 1951, in Biloxi. United States senator Lester C. Hunt (D-Wyo) presided over the proceeding to investigate the allegations of gambling and its effects on airmen stationed at the Biloxi air base. Among local individuals called to testify before the committee were Mayor R. Hart Chinn; Police Chief Earl F. Wetzel; Police Captain Louis Rosetti; City Commissioner A.J. Creel; Sheriff Laz Quave; Sheriff Luther Maples; Major General James F. Powell, commander, Keesler Field; C.P. Galle, Griffin McEachern and Pete Leonetti, pinball machine operators; John Bertucci; E.C. Tonsmeire, bank president; Val C. Redding, Greyhound bus station manager; Major Charles R. Alexander, base air police; and J.P. Coleman, state attorney general.

Keesler Airfield hangar area, Biloxi. *Courtesy of Mississippi Department of Archives and History.*

Keesler Airfield processing area, Biloxi. *Courtesy of Mississippi Department of Archives and History.*

Committee members gathered large amounts of incriminatory information during the hearings and subsequent investigation into the operation of illegal liquor and gambling establishments in proximity to the Biloxi airfield, where approximately thirty thousand airmen were stationed at the time. Harold Foreman, a United Press International correspondent, reported details of one of the hearings in a front-page article in *The Delta Democrat-Times* entitled "Slot Operator Tells of Paying Police":

> *A Biloxi slot machine operator testified at a Congressional hearing into wholesale gambling here today that he pays up to $700 in "fines" to Police Chief Earl Wetzel. Griffin McEachern was called during a sensational hearing by a Senate preparedness subcommittee that previously produced testimony that (1) Some airmen at Keesler Air Force Base pawned their uniforms and stole money to feed gambling devices in Harrison County where Biloxi and the huge base are located, (2) Losses ran up to $400,000 a month—one eighth of Keesler's payroll, and (3) There are almost 1,500 assorted gambling devices in the county, including slot machines, horse race wires, dice tables, and poker games.*

McEachern testified that he was the sole owner of Bay Novelty Company and had 64 machines in operation the previous week. He admitted that he paid a "fine" of $12.50 a month per machine, in cash, to Chief Wetzel, who gave him no receipts. Major Charles B. Alexander, air police officer at Keesler, and Downey Rice, committee counsel, submitted an inventory of gambling devices and paraphernalia listing 1,421 slot machines, 31 dice tables, 72 blackjack games, 55 poker tables and 11 race wires in Harrison County.

The Kefauver Crime Committee hearing and the investigation's findings revealed the existence of "a conspiracy by city and county officials to not only permit illegal gambling and alcohol to flourish on the Coast, but to use profits from the operations to load up government coffers." Although the committee publicized the results of a survey it conducted, reporting that more than 320 bars, supper clubs and other businesses may have been involved in the conspiracy, it seemed no immediate action to enforce the committee's findings took place at the time.

On February 4, 1952, a few months after McEachern testified at the October hearing, *The Delta Democrat-Times* reported a rumor of "racket busting" and Attorney General J.P. Coleman's plan to lead another raid on the Gulf Coast's "plush gambling and liquor joints." A follow-up article two weeks later reported that more rumors of an imminent raid on the Gulf Coast had erupted after Attorney General Coleman made a weekend visit to Biloxi about two weeks after he had led national guardsmen on a "surprise raid on two Coastal gambling establishments located within 10 feet of the Alabama state line." Coleman spoke publicly during his weekend trip, stating the Jackson County raid was "not a one-shot affair, but the first step in a statewide drive against lawbreakers and gamblers." Interestingly, Gulf Coast nightclubs closed their doors shortly after midnight each night during Coleman's weekend visit.

In March 1952, with the results of the well-documented and publicized Kefauver Crime Committee hearings still fresh in the minds of Biloxi's business community, Senator Howard McDonnell, along with Ernest Desporte, Albert Sidney Johnson, Frank P. Corso, Daniel Guice, William Dukate, William E. Beasley and Lynden Bowring, met with state legislators to discuss the issue of legalizing liquor. Their intent, a news article in Biloxi's *Daily Herald* reported, was to advocate and lobby for a "local option liquor bill." Also in March, Harold B. Knox, a United Press International correspondent, reported in *The Delta Democrat-Times* that state legislators had failed to pass "any laws of major consequence" during the first five weeks of the 1952 session. He also reported that "Senator Howard McDonnell of Biloxi was scheduled to toss in the first bill calling for repeal of the state's dry laws…McDonnell's bill [called for] local option with each county to decide…whether it wants legal liquor. All tax money collected would go into county, rather than state treasuries."

Local Option Vote Fails

Later in the 1952 legislative session, an act was passed calling for a referendum of the state's dry law. The referendum bill called for voters to decide whether they wanted a local option law or strict enforcement of statewide prohibition. In the months that preceded the election, scheduled for August 26, 1952, campaigns for a continuation of prohibition were well underway. *The Delta Democrat-Times* reported in its June 23, 1952 edition that state bootleggers were aligning themselves "with dry forces." A Jackson newspaper reported that United Drys began a grassroots campaign to defeat a local option proposal, and an editorial in the *Jackson Daily News* said bootleggers "will be working hand in hand with the United Drys, professional reformers, and church organizations that have declared against the proposal to legalize liquor, and they have their forces fully mustered to cast negative votes at the polls." The Jackson newspaper also stated that "defeat of the local-option proposal would be 'great victory' for bootleggers and moonshiners in counties where public sentiment favor legalized liquor."

It was no surprise in late August 1952 that many Mississippi residents who went to the polls voted to retain the state's dry law. Various news outlets published the election results, reporting the Gulf Coast and Delta counties heavily voted for local option. *The Delta Democrat-Times* reported that "the margin in favor of prohibition was roughly one and one-half to one." The same article also stated the dry vote was not expected to "curtail across-the-county liquor sales in city and county-licensed package stores and bars along the Gulf Coast and in cities on the Mississippi River." A front-page editorial in Jackson's *Clarion-Ledger* on the day after the election declared, "The peoples' mandate [to retain state prohibition] commands the legislature to strengthen statewide prohibition enforcement laws…this mandate is now binding on every single legislator. They asked for it." Governor Hugh White also weighed in on the referendum election, stating he considered enforcement to be the responsibility of local sheriffs and expected them to "dry up their individual areas of responsibility."

Local Crime Commission Appeals for Help

The Gulf Coast's problems with unlawful gambling and illegal liquor sales, however, did not end with the Kefauver Crime Committee or with the failed referendum election in August 1952. But national political pressure placed on state officials by the crime committee apparently did force local law enforcement to make a somewhat weak attempt to curtail crime along Mississippi's coastline. In early 1955, an attorney for the Harrison County Crime Commission asked Senate Democratic leader Lyndon Johnson to reopen the investigation started by the Kefauver Committee on "wide open gambling" near Keesler Air Force Base. A United Press article published in *The Delta Democrat-Times* on June 8, 1955, reported, "Thomas L. Wallace, attorney for the Harrison County Crime Commission, said his group has 'hit the end of the road' in efforts to stamp out 'flourishing lawlessness' along the Gulf Coast." Wallace explained to Senator Johnson that the only alternative remaining was to ask the Senate Armed Services and Preparedness Committee to reopen its 1951 investigation. Wallace's written request to Senator Johnson referred to the Gulf Coast area as it had been described in the Kefauver Crime Commission reports the year before as a place where "the streets were almost literally lined with slot machines." Wallace blamed Governor White and Harrison County officials for failing to follow through with enforcement actions against gambling after the National Guard raid in 1952. Also, Governor White "contended that local officials must enforce the state's rigid liquor and gambling laws." Interestingly, Wallace's appeal to clean up Biloxi and Harrison County specifically targeted illegal gambling, but it mentioned nothing about enforcement of the state's liquor law or closing down illegal liquor dealers.

GOVERNOR HUGH WHITE ORDERS RAID

In the months that followed, Harrison County citizens' groups continued with their complaints to Mississippi governor White, asking him to deal with rampant illegal activities occurring in the state's resort area. Finally, in early September 1952, the governor ordered fifty-four guardsmen to conduct a simultaneous raid on seven Gulf Coast establishments, where they "seized truckloads of whiskey and gambling equipment [from] ritzy nightspots." Twelve persons were arrested during the raid, and nearly two hundred cases of illegal liquor and gambling paraphernalia were seized. The *Anniston* (AL) *Star* reported that national guardsmen received "a secret briefing at an abandoned summer quarters near Biloxi," where the impending raid was staged, and "half a dozen newsmen flown from Jackson in a National Guard plane" were present when raid participants received their last-minute orders. The article also reported the raid signaled "a drive to clean up Gulf Coast lawlessness." Allegedly, the raid was planned with the utmost secrecy, but news of it must have leaked to several operators who stopped gambling activities and stowed away their equipment. Although no evidence of gambling was found at the Broadwater Beach Hotel restaurant, guard commander Wilson reported that "most of the loot," which included thirteen roulette, blackjack and dice tables, was seized from the Pines, "a plush gambling den just inside the Mississippi Louisiana border." The club had formerly operated as the Oasis and "provided shuttle bus service for patrons from New Orleans." Other nightclubs raided were Fairchild's, the Five O'Clock Club, Ray's Drive-In, the Shangri-La and Paradise Point.

Various news accounts reported that several truckloads of "illegal liquor and other illegal paraphernalia" were transported to a warehouse at the Mississippi Air National Guard training center, where guardsmen "smashed cases of liquor, champagne, and wines." Around 3:00 a.m., Colonel William C. Holmes "tossed a torch into a huge stack of gasoline drenched gambling equipment, touching off a blaze that burned for more than an hour," and promised to keep Gulf Coast "places clean of gambling." Colonel Holmes also stated, "I have orders to stay down here until gambling is broken on the Gulf Coast."

On September 8, 1952, *The Delta Democrat-Times* published a front-page account of the raid, a syndicated article written by H.L. Stevenson, who later served as UPI's managing editor. The news article reported the names of several individuals arrested as a result of the raid and charged with possession of gambling equipment and illegal liquor. Names listed in the article were John T. Fairchild and Theodore Wise at Fairchild's; Abel O'Cool and Mrs. Jonnie Parkinson at Shangri-La; Joe Simon Jr. at the Five O'Clock; Harold J. Zimmerman and Robert E. Moran at the Pines; Raymond E. Kidd, J.D. Horlock and M.G. Seunneau at Ray's; and Joe Astorias, originally from New York, and Charles Dunaway at Paradise Point. The article also reported that state adjutant general William P. Wilson announced "there will be no more wholesale raids but spot checks would be made of the dozens of places strung along more than 35 miles of the coastline." Overall, the 1952 raid seemed insignificant to many Gulf Coast owners and operators, and to a few observers, since a small number of liquor and gambling establishments were raided and a seemingly insignificant number of owners and operators were arrested. And business as usual soon returned with a vengeance. Some individuals began to believe the Dixie Mafia had grabbed a portion of the

Gulf Coast action, and resort area residents feared the Gulf Coast would never be the same.

Just months after he had ordered guardsmen to raid Harrison County liquor and gambling establishments and had confiscated illegal booze and gambling equipment, outgoing state governor Hugh White testified during a Federal Communications Commission (FCC) hearing held on January 10, 1956. The *Delta Democrat-Times* reported that Governor White appeared as a surprise character witness for Jimmy H. Love Jr., principal backer for Biloxi's proposed new television station, WLOX Channel 13, and owner of the Buena Vista Hotel. During his testimony, Governor White admitted that he knew Love sold liquor at his hotel. The governor argued, however, that Love was "a very progressive young, outstanding citizen of this state" and that Love was a "colonel on his staff." White added that it was his understanding that Gulf Coast hotels sold liquor because the resort area's residents wanted it because of the tourist trade. White added, "As a result of it [the tourist trade] there is no effort made on the part of the state government to break up the sale of liquor in this community which caters to the tourist trade."

AXES, BOOZE AND GAMBLING DEVICES

On January 17, 1956, just a week after outgoing governor White testified at the FCC hearing in Biloxi, James Plemon Coleman Jr. succeeded Governor White when he was sworn in as Mississippi's fifty-second governor. The new governor was no stranger to Mississippi politics, however, or to the state's liquor issue, since he had served as a circuit judge and as the state's attorney general. Within a few months of settling into the governor's mansion in downtown Jackson, the new governor convened a press conference at the mansion and publicly presented his policy on illegal alcohol. On May 22, 1956, *The Delta Democrat-Times* reported that Governor Coleman announced that Mississippi's bootleggers, like other violators, would have no immunity from the law. Noting that "different shades of attitude of the people concerning liquor in general" exist, the governor explained the constitution "commands the governor to uphold the law—and Mississippi has a prohibition law." Additionally, Governor Coleman addressed his policy concerning the state highway patrol's "relation to liquor laws" and explained the patrol was "not out hunting liquor but would enforce prohibition on highways in its jurisdiction."

Between 1956 and 1962, raids on restaurants and other nightspots continued throughout the Gulf Coast region, but gambling, instead of illegal liquor sales, seemed to be the driving force behind the enforcement actions. During 1961 alone, gambling paraphernalia, including slot machines, roulette wheels, blackjack tables and dice tables, was confiscated from almost a dozen Harrison County establishments. Biloxi's *Daily Herald* reported that Chez Joey's, Bennie French's, Eight Day Lounge, Hi-Hat Club, Gay Paree, Fiesta Club, Trader John's, Sea 'N Sirloin Restaurant, Cabana Beach Motel, Key Club and the Beverly Lounge were raided that year. Although the confiscation of illegal liquor was not mentioned in the article, little doubt exists that illegal liquor was sold in the clubs raided.

When Ross R. Barnett, a former trial lawyer and a staunch segregationist, was elected in 1959 as Mississippi's fifty-third governor, not only did he inherit the state's long-standing liquor issue, but he also assumed the state government's top seat in the midst of the civil rights movement. In 1962, just weeks before James Meredith became the first black student at the University of Mississippi in Oxford, Governor Barnett addressed what had become a decades-long pattern of illegal and criminal activities in one of the country's most popular conference and resort areas.

Former governor Ross Barnett and Mrs. Barnett at the Gubernatorial Ball, 1963. *Courtesy of Mississippi Department of Archives and History.*

The governor's enforcement effort began when he ordered the National Guard to carry out a raid planned for June 13, 1962, on more than one hundred Gulf Coast nightspots. Although the governor's order specifically targeted professional gambling clubs, most of the establishments raided also sold various types of illegal booze. The *Times-News*, of Hendersonville, North Carolina, published details of the well-publicized raid led by Major General W.P. Wilson in its next-day edition, stating that national guardsmen smashed gambling equipment with axes and destroyed "hundreds of bottles of liquor." Four arrests were made during the raids, and Governor Barnett proclaimed the raid was "just a sample" of action he planned to take "if professional gambling doesn't come to an abrupt halt in Mississippi." Harrison County sheriff Curtis O. Dedeaux requested one hundred or so nightspots that sell liquor to "close and remain closed until further notice." Although guardsmen allowed customers to leave the clubs raided, "operators were taken into custody." Barnett said, "I gave them an ultimatum in February—and I mean business when I talk. They are going to comply with what I say, and I don't want any pussyfooting." A UPI article in the Greenville newspaper presented another view of the raid:

> *If the shutdown continues, hundreds of persons will be out of jobs, and this area's economy—geared to the tourist trade—will be severely damaged. The state treasury will also suffer from a lack of "black market tax" revenue from illegal liquor sales. It was estimated that at least $25,000 worth of gambling equipment was destroyed at the Key Club, the Gay Paree and The Spot—all located along coastal U.S. 90 between here and Gulfport. There was no violence at any of the three clubs, raided simultaneously by teams of about 10 guardsmen each.*

Ray Bellande identified club owners mentioned in various news articles about the 1962 raids and posted the information on the Biloxi Historical Society website. Bernard A. Blaize owned the Gay Paree nightclub, and John Romeo owned the Key Club. Romeo and a patron named Jack N.S. Dennis were arrested during the raid. James L. Porter, identified as the owner of the Spot, was arrested at his club. Bellande further wrote, "Mr. Porter pleaded guilty to possession of gambling equipment and intoxicating liquor. He was fined $138, but $7500 of his gambling devices and paraphernalia were destroyed and $3000 was confiscated. Roger K. D'Angelo, an employee, was also arrested."

In an effort to fight back on behalf of his constituency in Harrison County, Sheriff Curtis O. Dedeaux lashed out at Governor Barnett for ordering the June raid as an effort to seek publicity for himself and his office. *The Delta Democrat-Times* reported the sheriff's sentiments, stating that Sheriff Dedeaux publicly complained that Governor Barnett could change nothing in a legally dry state by raiding Gulf Coast nightspots:

> *We don't give a damn how many raids he orders…A raid is a routine thing down here. We've been having them for years…He's not going to change anything on the coast and he knows it…I don't believe in going behind closed doors and looking for something without valid reason. People have rights…Barnett could have had all these places raided Wednesday night simply by giving me a call. But this would not have given him any publicity. He just wants newspaper clippings saying he had a raid.*

Throughout the rest of 1962 and during 1963, gambling operations resumed in more than a few Harrison County establishments. Just before Labor Day weekend, with thousands of tourists flocking to the Gulf Coast region for the end-of-the-season holiday, Governor Barnett sent a mandatory closure order via telegrams to five known gambling spots. On September 1, 1963, *The Delta Democrat-Times* reported that clubs and owners receiving telegrams were H.E. "Lefty" Blaize, the Gay Paree, West Beach, Biloxi; Jake McLandanich Sr., Jake McLandanich Jr. and John McLandanich, Fiesta Club, West Beach, Biloxi; John Romeo, the Key Club; the Spot Restaurant No. 6 Lounge, attention Mr. Porter, East Beach, Mississippi City; and Richard Head, Say When, West Beach, Biloxi.

Bars, Brothels and Benefactors

Events that occurred over the next few years explained why Dedeaux was angered by Governor Barnett's 1962 raid, and they confirmed what many Harrison County residents already knew about the sheriff. When Dedeaux warned Gulf Coast nightspots of the impending raid, he was protecting, at least in part, his own personal interests. Sheriff Dedeaux defended his post-raid comments in an article published in *Life* magazine soon after the event when he admitted, "If I tried to enforce the liquor laws, I'd bankrupt hundreds of businesses here. I'd cut the tourist trade by half [and then] the citizens would run me out of town." Although very little was known by the public in 1962 about Dedeaux's criminal activities, court documents and other historical records tell the story of his trouble-ridden years, beginning with his inauguration as Harrison County sheriff in 1960. Born in Harrison County on October 6, 1919, Dedeaux was a local businessman who earned a master's degree in political science from the University of Chicago. Prior to being elected sheriff, Dedeaux was employed at a local packing plant. His run for sheriff in 1959 was his second attempt to be elected to the office, and he narrowly defeated challenger Edward "Eddie" McDonnell, a former county sheriff, by fewer than one hundred votes. In retrospect, Dedeaux may have seen the county's chief law enforcement position as an opportunity to line his own pockets. It also seems likely that some of his supporters may have known from the start that he was open to accepting protection money from owners and operators of Harrison County's many illegal businesses.

The sheriff's troubles actually began when one of his benefactors, Joseph A. Garriga, developed his own problems with the law. Garriga and his brother, Edward, operated the Silver Dollar Lounge, a local bar and brothel, and in 1962, the brothers were charged with violating the White Slavery Act. During Joseph Garriga's trial, seven witnesses, including Garriga himself, testified that he paid protection money to Sheriff Dedeaux. In return, Garriga said, the sheriff promised to ensure the Silver Dollar Lounge, where he offered slot machines, illegal liquor and prostitution to his patrons, would remain open. The jury subsequently convicted Garriga and sentenced him to federal prison. Garriga's accusations against Dedeaux, however, soon became part of an ongoing investigation into allegations of the sheriff's own wrongdoings, including the discovery that Dedeaux failed to report his ill-gotten gains to the Internal Revenue Service. Subsequently, Dedeaux was

Curtis O. Dedeaux, former sheriff of Harrison County. *Courtesy of Ray Bellande, Gulf Coast historian.*

indicted by a federal grand jury, an event that cost him his position as sheriff. When the former sheriff's case went to trial, he was found guilty of filing false information on income tax returns. The judge sentenced Dedeaux to two years in federal prison and fined him $15,000. In an unfortunate twist of fate, the former Harrison County sheriff never made it to jail. An article published in Biloxi's *Daily Herald* reported that Curtis O. Dedeaux was found dead on September 10, 1966, at his residence on Oak Ridge Circle in West Biloxi. An autopsy was ordered, since Dedeaux died at home, and the results of the autopsy showed the official cause of the former sheriff's death was "poisoning due to an overdose of barbiturates."

Opening (and Closing) the Road to Corruption

In late 1965, two separate statements made by state senators W.B. Alexander of Cleveland and Howard McDonnell of Biloxi seemed to be preambles to discussion of the state's long-standing liquor issue. During a speech he made to the Leland Lions Club, Senator Alexander primarily focused on realignment of political districts in Mississippi and on the state's liquor issue. The Greenville newspaper reported the senator told attendees that Mississippi's illegal liquor trade was "ruining the moral fiber of the people of our state." He added that Mississippi was receiving approximately $4.2 million in revenue from taxes paid by 1,285 retail and 28 wholesale liquor dealers and explained that if legal liquor control laws were in place, the state likely would gain an additional $11 to $12 million in tax revenue. The newspaper quoted the senator as saying, "The liquor law now is too tempting to our officers, and it is destroying respect for our officers. Any child 10 or 12 years old can buy himself a fifth of whiskey in hundreds of places in the state." Alexander believed that Harrison County's Strip between Biloxi and Gulfport was an example of how illegal liquor fostered corruption that included organized prostitution, dope and gambling rings, further stating that a liquor control law "would clear up all that." On Sunday, December 26, 1965, *The Delta Democrat-Times* published a front-page article addressing issues of concern to Mississippi lawmakers during the upcoming year's legislative session, including Senator McDonnell's denouncement of state prohibition laws as "hypocritical" and his pledge to fight for legalization of liquor in the state. McDonnell claimed an "unholy alliance" of bootleggers and dry ministers had in the past kept the state legally dry, opening the road for corruption in counties in which illegal liquor was sold on a more or less open basis.

"A LITTLE APART FROM MISSISSIPPI"

Mississippi governors, *left to right*: Ross Barnett, J.P. Coleman, William Waller, John Bell Williams and Paul B. Johnson Jr. at the governor's mansion, Jackson, 1976. *Courtesy of Mississippi Department of Archives and History.*

In early 1966, the Gulf Coast continued business as usual, and along with tourism, liquor and gambling thrived. News reporter John F. Hussey chronicled the boom in Biloxi in a syndicated news article entitled "Gambling Business Booming in Biloxi," published in the *Bridgeport* (CT) *Telegram* on February 10, 1966. Hussey wrote about the uniqueness of the Mississippi Gulf Coast region and explained that "gambling is against the law in any form in Mississippi. And so is the sale of alcoholic beverages." In spite of the laws, he added, Mississippi's Gulf Coast was among the "most popular tourist and convention centers in the nation...a place where a man can buy a drink and roll a dice." He praised the resort area's "luxurious hotel and motel accommodations, fine food, good entertainment and Mississippi hospitality" and added that Biloxi was "second only to New Orleans as the biggest convention center from Miami to Galveston." The previous year, Hussey continued, Mississippi Gulf Coast tourism had brought nearly $80 million into the area. When he questioned Anthony Ragusin, Biloxi Chamber of Commerce director, about the absence of an official tax on area gambling, the chamber director replied, "We're against it." But Louis Rosetti, Biloxi police chief, provided a snapshot of illegal Gulf Coast activities when he admitted to Hussey that Biloxi and the surrounding vacation area had always been "a little apart from Mississippi" in the enforcement of liquor and gambling laws.

Chapter 11

A Liquor Storm Brewing

M ississippi's liquor issue long had been the subject of discussion and debate, both inside and outside the state capitol walls, and countless newspaper articles documented over five decades of liquor issues. One particular article, written by Kathy Lally and published in July 1966 in the *Baltimore Sun*, recounted an interview she conducted with Bill Minor, longtime journalist and former Mississippi bureau chief of the *New Orleans Times-Picayune*. Lally wrote that she considered Minor to be "the voice of conscience in Mississippi." During her interview with Minor, he referred to Mississippi as "a state of conundrums" and added, "State officials saw no reason not to reap a financial benefit from liquor that was sold in Louisiana and brought into Mississippi. The state set up a highly organized system, getting a copy of liquor shipments from the Louisiana Department of Revenue and showing up on the door of the Mississippi importer and demanding 10 percent. There was even an official stamp as proof of payment."

THE JACKSON COUNTRY CLUB RAID

Minor's statement about the financial benefit of liquor sales to Mississippi was indeed true. By 1966, the state was taking in an estimated $4.5 million in revenues generated from taxes paid by illegal liquor dealers, who allegedly operated businesses that brought in $36 million. Without a doubt, liquor dealers

Gubernatorial candidate Paul B. Johnson Jr. casts a vote in the 1963 election. *Courtesy of Mississippi Department of Archives and History.*

and the tax collector could not have been happier. But an illegal liquor storm that had been brewing for decades finally hit Mississippi on February 4, 1966, shortly after Governor Paul B. Johnson Jr. openly spoke out against the state's dry law. The eye of the storm was the fairly new Jackson Country Club, located just outside the city limits of Jackson. After the annual Carnival ball ended at a downtown Jackson hotel, revelers gathered at the posh, private club north of town for a post-coronation champagne toast and celebration in honor of the newly crowned Mardi Gras king and queen. Shortly after midnight, the celebration came to a halt when Hinds County deputy sheriffs charged into the club with sledgehammers and axes in hand. The *Lawton* (OK) *Morning Press* reported details of the raid in its February 6, 1966 edition:

> *Tom Shelton, Hinds County Acting Sheriff…and his axe-wielding helpers converged on the country club where the governor and Jackson society were toasting the Junior League Carnival Ball King and Queen. While startled society matrons and business leaders watched, the deputies uncovered case after case of liquor. "Paul, can't you do something about this?" said a woman in a full length mink to the governor. "I made my stand, I took my chance," replied Johnson.*

In the aftermath of the raid, club members asked one another if they knew the governor would be present. Acting Hinds County sheriff Tom Shelton, referred to by capital city club owners and bootleggers as the "Untouchable," overheard the questions and quickly explained the raid did not occur because of the governor's speech urging the legislature to pass a local option law. One reveler, who apparently drank too much champagne

Hinds County deputy sheriff Bill Russell confiscating champagne during the liquor raid at Jackson Country Club in February 1966. *Courtesy of Fred Blackwell.*

during the pre-raid celebration, shouted to officers carrying out cases of liquor, "Look, they're bringing us more." The Lawton newspaper article attempted to explain the remark, saying Mississippi law officers in the past have "reportedly supplied 'society events' with leftovers from confiscated whiskey." Others in the crowd began cursing as it became apparent that officers were confiscating the club's liquor inventory. One tuxedo-clad man tripped a deputy, who allegedly told the man in a polite voice, "I put you in jail once before for drunken driving," and arrested the man again. The confiscated liquor was transported by deputies to the Hinds County Courthouse, where it was to be inventoried. The Lawton newspaper article included an Associated Press photograph of two men identified as Hinds County deputy sheriff Tom Shelton and local insurance company executive George Gear.

A personal recollection of someone who witnessed the raid said deputies used sledgehammers to smash the door of the fairly large liquor storage room, where numerous cases of expensive champagne and other types of liquor were stored. Clad in a tuxedo, Governor Johnson witnessed the chaos and the carnage inside when he arrived at the club just minutes after lawmen left with the enormous cache of illegal liquor. Charles Wood, assistant club manager and an unexpected casualty of the raid, was charged with unlawful possession of liquor. A *Time* magazine article reported on Mississippi's long history of illegal liquor and included its version of the February raid, stating that Governor Johnson had urged Mississippians the week before the raid to repeal the prohibition law. "The hypocrisy of their back-door drinking habits, [the governor] told the legislature, makes Mississippians the 'laughingstock' of the nation." Johnson said, "It is high time for someone to stand boldly in the front door and talk plainly, sensibly and honestly about whiskey, black-market taxes, payola, and all of the many-colored hues that make up Mississippi's illegal aurora borealis of prohibition."

JUDGE BARBER RULES

The Jackson Country Club, believing its status as a private club protected it from the state's liquor law, soon filed a lawsuit on behalf of Charles Wood, the club's assistant manager charged with unlawful possession of liquor, a state felony. The case was assigned to County Judge Charles T. Barber's court, and the well-publicized trial took place during the 1966 legislative session. Interestingly, two Delta mayors were among the fairly large number of high-profile witnesses called to testify. When the mayor of Indianola, Mississippi, was asked on the witness stand if he "made any attempt to control liquor consumption in private homes," he responded, "No sir, we don't. I'm afraid I'd get caught." But the court heard a more telling revelation when Louis Munn, who served as mayor of Leland, admitted under oath that in his hometown, liquor dealers regularly pleaded guilty every two weeks and paid nominal fines. After four days of similar testimony from other witnesses, County Judge Barber threatened to order a strict enforcement of the prohibition ban statewide if the legislature chose to take no action to resolve the illegal liquor issue. Judge Barber based his statement on testimonies of witnesses in his courtroom who offered rather conclusive proof that Mississippi, a legally dry state, was, in reality, very wet. On April 6, 1966, *The Delta Democrat-Times* reported, "County Judge Charles T. Barber granted a motion to quash illegal possession 'charges' against Charles Wood, 42, assistant-club manager who was arrested during the raid. Barber also upheld arguments that the 1909 prohibition law had been 'rendered void by collecting state tax on liquor,'" and some believed the landmark decision could have a far-reaching effect throughout the state.

LOCAL OPTION LAW BECOMES EFFECTIVE

During the week that followed the country club raid, newspapers and magazines throughout the country repeatedly published articles about Mississippi's prohibition law. One of these articles appeared in the February 11, 1966 edition of *Time* magazine and reminded its readers of Mississippi's liquor history, saying, "The drys have their law, the wets have their whiskey and the state gets its taxes," and further explained that drinkers "had no problem" buying alcohol in fifty-nine of the state's eighty-two counties. The article added that Johnson "has in mind a state-run distribution system similar to that in Washington State…which with approximately the same population collected $42 million in liquor taxes last year. Johnson proposed to earmark the extra funds for the state's inadequate school system and public health services." The article indicated that tourists and conventioneers who preferred not to break alcohol laws "would probably be more numerous… Since whiskey is a high-proof issue in Mississippi, Johnson did not ask the legislators—who do their drinking in 'private clubs' in Jackson—to repeal

Mississippi governor Paul B. Johnson signs the local option law, effectively ending state prohibition. *Courtesy of McCain Library Digital Archives, University of Southern Mississippi.*

the law on their own. Instead, he asked them to authorize a referendum by March 15."

Without a doubt, embarrassment created by the raid on a country club whose members were socially prominent and politically well connected had an impact on the legislature's efforts over the next few weeks to revisit the state's liquor law. Within a few weeks, the Mississippi legislature passed a local option bill allowing counties to hold referendum elections and vote "yes" or "no" to the sale of liquor within their jurisdictions. On May 21, 1966, during a history-making event in the state of Mississippi, Governor Paul B. Johnson Jr. signed the local option bill into law. The measure became effective less than two months later, on July 1, 1966. To many, it seemed the conflict between governmental sanity and expediency finally had ended.

Chapter 12

It's Legal—Now What?

In the weeks prior to July 1, 1966, most Mississippi bootleggers and others who sold and distributed illegal bonded liquor faced the huge reality of losing millions of dollars in income. Although liquor sales soon could become legal if county residents chose to hold referendum elections to determine their area's wet or dry status, the new law imposed a two-week moratorium on liquor sales by dealers and bootleggers. If these individuals violated the moratorium, they would be denied the opportunity to apply for a state license to sell liquor in a wet county. A few county sheriffs met with bootleggers to explain this particularly unpopular portion of the law. One local newspaper, the *Holmes County Herald*, reported that Holmes County sheriff Andrew Smith had met with a majority of local bootleggers, and "most of them" had agreed to comply with the two-week requirement in order to become eligible for a liquor license. The sheriff added that most dealers and bootleggers indicated they planned to apply for the license. Enforcement responsibility for the newly passed law was delegated to the county's highest elected official, the sheriff. State enforcement, however, became the responsibility of a new entity, the Alcoholic Beverage Control board, and state alcohol agents, who were armed and vested with arrest authority, would be tasked with investigating alleged violations of Mississippi's alcohol laws.

The Gulf Coast Celebrates

As all Gulf Coast residents and other interested parties expected, a referendum election was held soon after the new law became effective on July 1, 1966, making Harrison County, with its cities of Biloxi and Gulfport, the first county in the state to put the new law into practice. And as a surprise to absolutely no one, Harrison County's vote was a resounding "wet." Legitimate businesses catering to the state's heavy tourist industry, particularly along the Mississippi Gulf Coast, also celebrated the long-awaited legalization of liquor sales. One of the best-documented of these celebrations was held at the Broadwater Beach Hotel, a large and well-known resort property in Biloxi. The *Reading* (PA) *Eagle* reported on the elaborate and boisterous scene in an Associated Press article published on July 18, 1966. Police cruisers, "with sirens screaming and lights flashing, escorted the big truck into Biloxi. The van sped to the plush Broadwater Beach Hotel, where a crowd cheered when the truck's rear doors were opened, revealing 77 cases [of liquor.]" Waiters carried the liquor into the hotel, where Louis Cobb chose a bottle of Scotch whiskey, poured a drink and offered it to T.M. Dorsett, the hotel's manager. As floodlights glared and photographs were taken, Mayor Dan Guice and county supervisor Laz Quave cut a ribbon stretched across the entrance to the lounge, and Dorsett downed "the first legal drink of whiskey poured in Mississippi after 58 years of prohibition, which never did work. The Gulf Coast, particularly, never paid attention to prohibition." Mayor Guice told attendees that legal liquor "will be a boon to our tourist industry and industrialization as well as removing the hypocritical attitude the state has had toward whiskey." After hotel manager Dorsett announced that drinks were on the house, three cases of liquor were consumed in record time. One individual remarked, "It still tastes the same, but somehow it seems better because it's legal." The article explained that although prohibition in the state of Mississippi had ended effective July 1, 1966, it had taken twenty-seven days for the state to put the machinery in place to legally sell whiskey.

Almost sixty years after Mississippi had enacted its own prohibition law, liquor sales on the Gulf Coast were officially legal. Seven counties in the state had already approved legal liquor sales, and more were scheduled to vote on the issue within a few days. To no one's surprise, three of Biloxi's most popular hotels and resorts—the Broadwater Beach, the Edgewater Gulf and the Buena Vista—were the first in the state of Mississippi to receive liquor licenses. The new law allowed "liquor by

Broadwater Beach Hotel, circa 1960, where Gulf Coast residents in 1966 celebrated the end of state prohibition. *Courtesy of Mississippi Department of Archives and History.*

the drink," but permits would be issued only in areas designated by the state as resorts. Fortunately, each of the three large properties was located within the designated resort area. Liquor was legal, and as history would determine in later years, hotels, businesses and entertainment venues along Mississippi's Gulf Coast would never look back.

Red Hydrick's Take

In Rankin County on what once had been the thriving Gold Coast, one of the state's most infamous bootleggers, Red Hydrick, waited to hear what he expected was bad luck for his illegal liquor business: news about the bill before the Mississippi legislature that certainly would change his life and livelihood. In the days before lawmakers voted "yes" to the law that effectively ended almost six decades of prohibition, Hydrick was interviewed by an Associated Press reporter. The aging bootlegger's take on the new local option law was published in numerous newspapers around the country, including the May 15, 1966 edition of the *Cochocton* (OH) *Tribune*. "Hearing the news the Mississippi Legislature voted Friday to end a half-century of prohibition, Red Hydrick of rural Rankin County said: 'I've been in the

G.W. "Red" Hydrick says goodbye to Gold Coast liquor customers, July 1, 1966. *Courtesy of Fred Blackwell.*

liquor business 40 years. I am in favor of legislation only if the state will keep its damn nose out of the business.'"

The *Hattiesburg* (MS) *News* reported that "bootleggers stashed their wares until counties could vote wet." Red Hydrick, "probably the best-known bootlegger in central Mississippi...sat in his bootlegger shack on the banks of the muddy Pearl River in Rankin County across from Jackson...surveyed the bare, unpainted wooden shelves, two empty bourbon bottles and rasped: 'I've been in this building 27 years and I've gone through hell. There has been a lot of money taken in through the front door of this shack, but through the hazards of this racket, there has been a lot go out the back door.'" Hydrick concluded with saying that he was "closing up" and "had made no plans for the future."

New Law, New Rules

A few months after the local option law became effective, *Time* magazine published another article that described some of the new law's anticipated effects, including increases in prices as "retailers—more than a third of them ex-bootleggers—boosted their markups. Bootleggers who stuck to bootlegging soon discovered that state and local governments no longer condone—or tax—smuggled booze. For the first time, convictions are being rigorously sought and obtained against purveyors of illegal liquor, and moonshine—which many Southerners prefer to the aged, taxed variety—is no longer so easy to buy. Biggest gainer is the state government, which expects to see alcohol revenues jump from $4,500,000 a year to more than $10 million." With local option laws newly in place, a one-day meeting of liquor license holders was held in Jackson. Called by a group interestingly known as Mississippians for Legal Counsel, Inc., the meeting's keynote speaker was Governor Paul B. Johnson Jr. A syndicated news article published on December 1, 1966, reported a portion of the governor's address to the group:

> *We have a law that was enacted in the best tradition of representative government and today—a majority of voters in 42 counties containing over 70 percent of Mississippi's people—have already voted for legal control of alcoholic beverages…You now have the responsibility of upholding the trust placed in you by the voters in your counties. They voted to try your way. They voted you in business. They can vote you out of business…you are the ones who will lose—immediately—if there is any loss of respect for this law.*

Bill Minor Remembers Prohibition

Years later, longtime journalist Bill Minor wrote about some of the events that occurred during the fifty-eight years of prohibition in Mississippi, including some that shaped the future of alcohol sales after 1966:

> *It took 58 years to get rid of Mississippi's farcical, corrupt statewide prohibition law, and ironically, a liquor raid on the posh Country Club of Jackson in February, 1966, triggered its doom. A conscientious new acting*

sheriff in town named Tom Shelton was told to clamp down on enforcing the law in Hinds County when he was moved up from chief deputy after irate local judges forced out the incumbent sheriff who stayed soused most of the time. So where does he start but at the high end of the social scale, the new country club, and for the premiere social event of the season, the Mardi Gras party for the 1966 Carnival King, leading industrialist, Warren Hood…One touch of irony the night of the raid: Jackson Mayor Allen Thompson was on his way when he heard on his police radio that the raid was underway, so he turned around and headed home…Paul Johnson, who in his long political career had run as a "dry," and was heavily influenced by the staunchly prohibitionist Hederman family, who owned the state's two largest newspapers in Jackson, stunned state legislators by advocating unabashedly the legalization of liquor. Saying "Mississippi… is a laughing stock of the nation as far as its so-called prohibition farce is concerned," Johnson added that "bootleggers and criminal elements are doing big business…and the state is in bed with them by taxing an illegal commodity."…What came out of the Legislature by late May was a unique system allowing counties to vote in legal sales of liquor by package stores with the State Tax Commission as the monopoly wholesaler statewide. That would be a big switch: from a state that for a half century prohibited booze to one that would now become its sole distributor.

Chapter 13

Alcoholic Beverage Control

The Mississippi Local Option Beverage Control Law, commonly known as local option, was signed on May 21, 1966, and the law went into effect on July 1, 1966. One of the provisions of the new law called for the establishment of the Alcoholic Beverage Control (ABC) Division, which effectively occurred on May 31, 1966, when Earl Evans Jr. was appointed director. In the weeks that followed, staff members were hired and warehouse space was leased. On October 11, 1966, Dr. A.V. Beacham was appointed director, and Mr. Evans began work as administrative assistant to the State Tax Commission. When the State Tax Commission filed its first annual report with the office of Governor Paul B. Johnson Jr. on December 28, 1967, the ABC Enforcement Division was staffed with twenty-six agents and two secretaries. Recruitment of ten additional agents and another secretary was planned during the next reporting period.

Mississippi's law stated that "alcoholic beverage means any alcoholic liquid, including distilled spirits, native wines and wine of more than 5% alcohol by weight, capable of being consumed by a human being. The term does not include wines of 5% or less of alcohol by weight and beer containing not more than 5% alcohol by weight pursuant to Miss. Code Ann. Section 67-1-5." A website maintained by the ABC defines its enforcement responsibility as "maintaining fair and equitable enforcement of the Local Option laws, the prohibition laws, and state beer laws in the state of Mississippi." Additional information posted on the ABC website reports that moonshine stills are routinely discovered, and subsequently destroyed, in various places throughout the state, adding, "Since 1966, ABC agents have successfully prosecuted in excess of 40,000 liquor law violations and destroyed approximately 3,000 illicit whiskey stills." In early 1967, the newly formed ABC Enforcement Division conducted its first raid in an "announced crackdown on untaxed liquor and gambling" when agents stormed into the small north Mississippi town of Grenada overnight on February 10–11. An account of the raid appeared in the mid-week edition of a south Mississippi newspaper, the *Hattiesburg American*. Interestingly, Chief L.R. Mashburn, identified in the article as the head of ABC's Enforcement Division, had served as Rankin County sheriff between 1948 and 1952.

> *The Alcoholic Beverage Control division Tuesday opened its war on gambling and illegal liquor with raids on three establishments in Grenada County. Agents seized almost 500 cases of beer and smashed 11 slot machines. Enforcement Chief L.R. Mashburn said agents raided the Grenada Country Club, Moose Club, and VFW Lodge. They smashed 10 slot machines at Moose Lodge and one at the country club, he said. They confiscated about 280 cases of beer at the Moose Lodge, 185 cases at the VFW club and 14 at the country club. It was taken to the state liquor warehouse in Jackson to be sold.*

Mississippi's local option law can be tricky to new residents and to non-residents who travel within the state. Technically, it is illegal to possess alcohol in a dry county, since state prohibition law still prevails. Thus, a hypothetical road trip from a location in a wet county either through or into a dry county just might mean breaking the law if liquor is present in the vehicle. For example, if an individual leaves a wet county en route to an event in another wet county, he or she may be stopped by law enforcement and charged with illegal liquor possession while driving through a dry county. Strange, but true.

ABC AGENTS AND ENFORCEMENT ACTIVITIES

Later in 1970, ABC agents raided a family-operated moonshine still near Byram, Mississippi, a small Hinds County town located south of Jackson. Exactly a year later, on February 15, 1968, *The Delta Democrat-Times* reported that five persons were arrested by authorities during "raids on moonshine whiskey stills in Yazoo, Madison, and Rankin Counties." All three counties were identified as dry areas. The news article identified the men arrested as "Johnnie Leflore, 43 of

Early ABC agents Bill Bailey and Larry Brewer during a raid of an illegal moonshine operation in 1970 near Byram, Mississippi. *Courtesy of Fred Blackwell.*

Bentonia; Frank Pierce, 50, and Willie Earl Pierce, 19, both of Canton; John Grant, 52, of the Luckney Community; and an unidentified 17 year old, also of Rankin County." The account concluded by stating, "Raids on the four illegal distilleries turned up more than 4,000 gallons of mash." During this same period in early 1968, former Scott County constable Wilbur Bates was arrested by Scott County sheriff Clell Harrell after he confiscated two gallons of moonshine from the constable's car. Allegedly, Bates was on his way to deliver the liquor. Shortly after the constable's arrest, Bates resigned from his position and posted a $1,000 bond, pending a hearing scheduled for a later date in a Scott County justice of the peace court.

Retired ABC alcohol agent and captain of Mississippi's northern division Keith Roberts recalled that ABC agents, on some occasions, called on federal agents to help them snare repeat violators in counties where local law enforcement was ineffective. Roberts explained that assistance was sought from federal alcohol agents since violators they arrested more often paid larger fines and served some time in federal prison. An example of using federal laws to enforce liquor laws was a 1970 case involving an Attala County sheriff, his deputy and five others who were indicted by a federal grand jury in Aberdeen, Mississippi. General John N. Mitchell announced that sealed indictments had been opened in U.S. District Court in Aberdeen charging Sheriff William B. Montague, Deputy Sheriff Woodrow W. Steen and five other individuals with violation of federal liquor laws by conspiring to operate an illegal still. All seven individuals were charged with conspiring to sell illegal moonshine whiskey in three southern states, including Mississippi.

Rusty Hanna, assistant executive director of the ABC Enforcement Division in Gluckstadt, Mississippi, explained the division has nine "Post of Duties" offices, divided into five districts. District I includes Jackson and Greenwood; District II, Senatobia and Tupelo; District III, Columbus and Meridian; District IV, Hattiesburg and Brookhaven; and District V, Biloxi. Hanna, who initially worked as an alcohol agent himself, confirmed that ABC agents are armed and well trained to deal with unexpected and potentially dangerous situations. A large portion of an agent's enforcement work involves investigating leads, locating moonshine stills, conducting raids and documenting enforcement cases with various types of information and photos of stills and apparatus confiscated. Under Mississippi liquor laws, manufacturing liquor for personal consumption is not a crime, but selling the substance is against the law. Although a small percentage of stills confiscated in current-day Mississippi can produce many gallons of alcohol, most moonshine stills discovered during twenty-first-century raids are limited in size and use rather crude equipment. One thing is certain—Mississippi's topography, much of it remote, hilly and heavily wooded, remains an ideal natural environment for protecting contemporary bootleggers, their stills and the moonshine they make. And certainly, no one can argue that ABC agents do not have a difficult and dangerous job.

The Alcoholic Beverage Control Division also serves as the state's sole liquor distributor and purchases various types of liquor through its office, which is overseen by the Mississippi State Tax Commission. According to the State Tax Commission's website, the ABC as the "state's wholesaler... imports, stores, and sells 2,850,000 cases of spirits and wines annually from its 211,000 square foot warehouse located in South Madison County Industrial Park…[and] offers Mississippi's 1,600 licensed retailers almost 5,000 brands and sizes of beverage alcohol…the 27.5% markup (set by state laws) on products shipped by the Warehouse yields some $58,000,000 of the $95,000,000 deposited annually into the state's General Fund."

Afterword

Without a doubt, passage of a local option law paved the way for more relaxed approaches to alcohol in present-day Mississippi. But what is the back story behind twenty-first-century attitudes in the state? Two reasons may account for the changes: the ages of the state's residents and the ever-evolving contemporary value system of our society today. It seems that twenty-one- to fifty-year-olds are less at odds with society's mores and religious convictions than people who lived during state prohibition. While drinking was once considered sinful according to Protestant-based teachings, and still is prohibited in some religious affiliations, beer and wine and even mixed drinks today seem to be well tolerated in a variety of social settings. It's no longer unusual to see champagne, wine and beer served at wedding receptions and other social gatherings, although these events primarily occur outside the walls of local Protestant churches or fundamental religious groups' social halls.

In 2013, the official ABC map indicated that thirty-two of Mississippi's eighty-eight counties were dry, meaning that residents also voted against advertising, production, sales, distribution and transportation of alcohol within the county's borders. Four counties—Chickasaw, Hinds, Jasper and Jones—were split between wet and dry. In one of those four counties, Hinds, where the state's capital city of Jackson is located and where hundreds of state and federal government employees work and live, citizens in the western half of the county voted wet and those who live in the eastern half voted dry. Although Madison County, where the burgeoning cities of Ridgeland

and Madison are located, is wet, in Rankin County, just a short drive across Spillway Road from Ridgeland, and where some of the former Gold Coast liquor dealers earned small fortunes during state prohibition, residents have voted dry since the initial local option election in 1966. In recent years, however, some civic leaders, local politicians and commercial developers have pushed for "liquor by the drink" in dry Rankin County, stating that hotels and restaurants need liquor sales to make a profit in today's economy. On January 23, 2014, after several years of discussion, debate and deliberation, a small turnout of Rankin County residents overwhelmingly voted to allow liquor by the glass in restaurants located on the heavily populated Rankin County side of the thirty-three-thousand-acre Ross Barnett Reservoir. In advance of the recent liquor vote, the cities of Brandon, Flowood and Pearl approved resort status for portions of Rankin County that border the water. It seems demographics haven't been the only change in central Mississippi; overall attitudes about liquor are evolving, as well.

Times have indeed changed. Although many of us who grew up in Mississippi during the '50s and '60s could not have imagined a distillery in our home state, one now exists. Mississippi's first legal liquor distillery since prohibition began, Cathead Vodka, occupies prime business space in Gluckstadt, a bustling Madison County enclave that is also home to Mississippi's ABC Commission. The distillery is co-owned by Richard Patrick and Austin Evans, and it produces several flavors of vodka, including honeysuckle and pecan. The Cathead brand is popular in Mississippi and elsewhere, although interstate shipping to some states is still limited by law. Cathead Vodka is a name to watch, as Patrick and Evans continue to grow the brand and market the distillery as a destination location in Madison County.

Another first happened in Mississippi on July 1, 2013—brewing beer at home became legal. Mississippi's Matt Berman wrote an article about craft beer that appeared in the July 3, 2013 online version of *National Journal*. Berman explained that after craft beer's "years of painful battles," brewing beer at home finally became legal in all fifty states. He explained, "Victory came when recently passed legislation that permits home-brewing in the last bastion of home sobriety, Mississippi, went into effect July 1—just three days before Independence Day." Prior to that date, brewing one's own beer at home was illegal in Mississippi. Jake McGraw, editor of Rethink Mississippi and policy coordinator at the William Winter Institute for Racial Reconciliation in Oxford, believes that Mississippi is "still lagging in the beer making industry." McGraw's article entitled "Baptists,

Bootleggers, and Brewmeisters: Mississippi's Entry into the Craft Beer Movement," posted to his website on November 1, 2013, included some facts about southern breweries:

> *Only three breweries operated in Mississippi in 2012, amounting to only one brewery per 1 million Mississippians—compared to one per 500,000 Alabamians, one per 200,000 Tennesseans, and, remarkably, one per 25,000 Vermonters, the country's sudsiest citizens. But thanks to a policy shift and a handful of entrepreneurial brewmeisters, 2013 has turned into a banner year for Mississippi's fledgling beer making industry. Since January the Magnolia State has welcomed at least five new craft breweries, the small, independent producers that generally favor bolder flavors and higher alcohol content.*

Mississippi's first craft brewery operates under the very southern-sounding name of Lazy Magnolia. The company's website tells the story of the brewery, started by Mark and Leslie Henderson in 2006. Touted as the state's oldest "packaging brewery," Lazy Magnolia is located in Kiln, Mississippi, near the Gulf Coast resort area. Interestingly, the idea for the popular brewery began rather innocently in 2003, when Leslie Henderson purchased a brewmaking kit as a Christmas gift of last resort for her husband, Mark. But it was Leslie's own interest in conquering the very old tradition of making homebrew that began a journey that culminated with the beer named Lazy Magnolia. Most beer types sold under the Lazy Magnolia label have names that are reminiscent of the South, including honeysuckle, pecan and a new special release dark brew named Old Money, part of the brewery's new Debutante Series. Currently, the brewery produces various types and flavors of beer that are available in over a dozen states.

And the wet Gulf Coast is even wetter than it was during state prohibition, thanks to the state's gaming laws and the presence of big-name, world-class casinos. Not only is gambling allowed, but alcoholic drinks are also free to gamblers. After years of battling illegal gambling in the state, particularly along the coast, the State of Mississippi now promotes the Gulf Coast region on its "official tourism site," www.visitmississippi.org, as "the third largest gaming destination in the U.S." If an individual chooses to buy beer, wine or other forms of alcohol in what once was known as "wettest dry state in the United States," it can be purchased legally in a majority of the state's counties. A look today at the names and locations of the state's dry counties reveals a pattern reminiscent of locations where the least illegal alcohol sales existed prior to 1966. Then and now, the wet counties along the Mississippi River, in the Delta region and along the Gulf Coast outnumber all other wet counties in the state. And after more than a century now, three of the underlying reasons for this pattern remain the same: religion, tourism and, of course, politics.

2013 Mississippi Code, Title 67—Alcoholic Beverages

Chapter 1—Local Option Alcoholic Beverage Control

§ 67-1-9—Alcoholic beverages prohibited except as authorized in this chapter; penalties

Universal Citation: MS Code § 67-1-9 (2013)

(1) It shall be unlawful for any person to manufacture, distill, brew, sell, possess, import into this state, export from the state, transport, distribute, warehouse, store, solicit, take order for, bottle, rectify, blend, treat, mix or process any alcoholic beverage except as authorized in this chapter. However, nothing contained herein shall prevent importers, wineries and distillers of alcoholic beverages from storing such alcoholic beverages in private bonded warehouses located within the State of Mississippi for the ultimate use and benefit of the State Tax Commission as provided in Section 67-1-41. The commission is hereby authorized to promulgate rules and regulations for the establishment of such private bonded warehouses and for the control of alcoholic beverages stored in such warehouses. Additionally, nothing herein contained shall prevent any duly licensed practicing physician or dentist from possessing or using alcoholic liquor in the strict practice of his profession, or prevent any hospital or other institution caring for sick and diseased persons, from possessing and using alcoholic liquor for the treatment of bona fide patients of such hospital or other institution. Any

drugstore employing a licensed pharmacist may possess and use alcoholic liquors in the combination of prescriptions of duly licensed physicians. The possession and dispensation of wine by an authorized representative of any church for the purpose of conducting any bona fide rite or religious ceremony conducted by such church shall not be prohibited by this chapter.
(2) Any person, upon conviction of any provision of this section, shall be punished as follows:
(a) By a fine of not less than One Hundred Dollars ($100.00), nor more than Five Hundred Dollars ($500.00), or by imprisonment in the county jail not less than one (1) week nor more than three (3) months, or both, for the first conviction under this section.
(b) By a fine of not less than One Hundred Dollars ($100.00) nor more than Five Thousand Dollars ($5,000.00) or by imprisonment in the county jail not less than sixty (60) days, nor more than six (6) months, or both fine and imprisonment, for the second conviction for violating this section.
(c) By a fine of not less than One Hundred Dollars ($100.00) nor more than Five Thousand Dollars ($5,000.00) or by imprisonment in the State Penitentiary not less than one (1) year, nor more than five (5) years, or both fine and imprisonment, for conviction the third time under this section for the violation thereof after having been twice convicted of its violation.

Appendix II

Liquor Lexicon

BATHTUB GIN: A poorly made homemade gin that was preferably served in a bottle so tall that it could not be mixed with water from a sink tap and, therefore, was mixed in a bathtub instead. Although the phrase specifically references gin, it became used as a general term for any type of cheap, homemade booze.

BLIND PIG: An illegal drinking establishment, aka speakeasy, that attempted to evade police detection by charging patrons a fee to gaze upon some sort of exotic creature (i.e., a blind pig) and be given a complimentary cocktail upon entrance. Also referred to as a "blind tiger."

BLOTTO: Extremely drunk, often to the point of unconsciousness.

BRICK OF WINE: Oenophiles looking to get their vino fix could do so by simply adding water to a dehydrated block of juice, which would become wine.

DRY: A noun used in reference to a man or woman who is opposed to the legal sale of alcoholic beverages. Bureau of Prohibition agents were often referred to as "dry agents." As an adjective, it describes a place where alcohol is not served.

GIGGLE WATER: Slang for any type of alcoholic beverage, alluding to the premise that alcohol causes some drinkers, particularly women, to giggle.

Apparently dating back to the '20s and '30s, this is surely a term that would be categorized today as discriminatory to females.

HOOCH: Low-quality liquor, usually moonshine or corn whiskey. The term originated in the late 1800s as a shortened form of "hoochinoo," a distilled beverage that became popular in Alaska during the Klondike gold rush. The word reappeared in the 1920s and became heavily used during Prohibition.

JAKE WALK: A paralysis or loss of muscle control in the hands or feet due to an overconsumption of Jamaican gin, aka "Jake," a legal substance with an alcoholic base. The numbness led sufferers to walk with a distinct gait that was also known as "Jake leg" or "Jake foot."

JUICE JOINT: A term for an illegal drinking establishment.

OMBIBULOUS: A term made up by writer H.L. Mencken to describe his love of alcohol; Mencken noted, "I'm ombibulous. I drink every known alcoholic drink and enjoy them all." Mencken was also fond of referring to bootleggers as "booticians" and is alleged to have invented the term "boozehound."

SKID ROAD: A precursor to the term "skid row." A skid road was the place where loggers hauled their goods. During Prohibition, these "roads" became popular meeting places for bootleggers to share their wares.

STERNO OR "CANNED HEAT": The jellied material sold in a can consisted of ethanol, an industrial alcohol, and potentially poisonous chemicals added to make it burn longer. After the contents of the can were filtered through a material such as a man's sock or ladies' hosiery, the resulting substance, rumored to cause blindness, often was used on the street as an alcohol substitute.

TEETOTALER: A person who abstains from alcohol consumption. The phrase likely originated in pre- and post-prohibition-era temperance societies and groups. The word was formed from the adding of a "T" to their signatures to indicate total abstinence from alcohol (T+total-ers).

WET: The opposite of dry, a wet is a person who favors the legal sale of alcoholic beverages or a location where liquor is openly sold.

WHALE: A heavy drinker.

WHITE LIGHTNING: The whiskey equivalent of bathtub gin. The substance was illegally made, very potent and often of poor quality.

WIDE OPEN: A term used to describe a location where illegal activities such as liquor sales, gambling and prostitution operated openly without fear of law enforcement actions.

Statistics Relating to Alcohol Production and Consumption

S tatistics from *American Prohibition Year Book for 1910*, edited by Charles R. Jones, Alonzo E. Wilson and Fred D.L. Squires (Chicago: Lincoln Temperance Press, 1910).

1. In 1909, alcohol-related health, family relationships and economic problems existed in 5 million households.
2. In 1920, the U.S. topped the list for alcohol consumption in the world (approximately 1.9 billion gallons of beer, wine, and other alcohol), with the United Kingdom and Russia ranked in 2nd and 3rd places.
3. In the year ended June 30, 1908, farmers produced 4,166,013,000 bushels of barley, wheat, rye, corn, and oats, and 300,368,805 bushels of these grains went into the liquor making business. Therefore, liquor making was considered advantageous to the farming economy in the United States.
4. In 1910, Mississippi had a total of 678 liquor distributors, including 15 wholesale distributors.
5. The total population of Mississippi in 1909 was 2.2 million.
6. Registered voters in Mississippi in 1909 total 77,738.

A Modern Take on "Local Option"

By Bill Minor

*Originally posted on djournal.com (*Northeast Mississippi Daily Journal*), March 9, 2000*

NEW LIQUOR BILL REVIVES MEMORY OF RANKIN BOOTLEGGERS

JACKSON—Self-respecting bootleggers from the days of Rankin County's "Gold Coast," the largest dispensers of booze during the heyday of Mississippi prohibition, would be horrified to learn there's talk of making hard liquor LEGAL by the drink in their one-time fiefdom. The legendary territory of illegal hooch dealers Casey's Lane and Old Fannin Road are now within the confines of the upstart Town of Flowood, which emerged almost from nowhere in recent years on the east side of Pearl River across from the Capital city of Jackson. Even when Mississippi finally ended its fantasy-land of statewide prohibition in 1966, Rankin County, which had been the biggest purveyor of contraband booze, voted to remain dry. Only beer and what is facetiously called light wine have recently been okayed. But now Flowood in reality a thriving segment of the Jackson metro area wants to come out from under the countywide liquor ban so that hard stuff by the drink could be legally sold with food in its growing restaurant and hotel industry. So far, Flowood's plan has won passage in the state Senate in a carefully crafted piece of legislation drawn to fit only the Rankin County village into Mississippi's overall Alcoholic Beverage Control Law. Of course, diners in Flowood hotels or restaurants can't get cocktails with their meals until the whole idea is approved by a majority of town voters. Specifically, the legislation mandates there could be no ABC-licensed package stores inside the municipality. The Gold Coast on the East Bank of the muddy Pearl across from Jackson got its name in pre–World War II days where gambling casinos as well as booze ran wide open, with a ready-made clientele of fun-starved folks out of the capital city, including state lawmakers. Slots, gaming tables and bars disappeared by the end of the war, but a healthy bootleg trade survived, with bonded whiskey sold in brown paper sacks out of the back door of "grocery stores" and tin-roofed clapboard shacks. There was always a heavy traffic of thirsty Jacksonians travelling across the old Woodrow Wilson Bridge over Pearl River knowing exactly the building where their favorite 'legger kept his goods. A well-used dirt driveway took them around the back of the joint and after a quick transaction a black guy handed the customer his fifth or pint of bonded stuff in a paper sack. A whole generation of Mississippians grew up thinking Old Charter was the only bourbon whiskey, since "Charter" was usually the only choice of brands. Some Mississippians still remember the state's "black market tax" which was collected with remarkable precision on illegal booze brought into the state, the great bulk from Louisiana which levied only a minimal tax on "export" liquor going out-of-state. Through an arrangement with Louisiana (first installed by then State Tax Collector William Winter) Mississippi got a copy of every invoice of whiskey headed into this state. Of course, the big Mississippi "wholesale" bootleggers were importing the great bulk of the hard stuff. Who should show up in the black market tax collection records as the highest volume importers? The operators in good old "dry" Rankin County. A book I was given a few years ago *Big Red*, a biography of notorious Rankin County bootlegger G.W. "Red" Hydrick gives a romanticized version of how the liquor traffickers operated and eluded local law enforcement whenever officers took a notion to crack down. Once when a reform sheriff came into office, Hydrick first devised a system of hiding his hooch in waterproof bags in the Pearl River. When that was discovered, next he had his helpers dig several holes in the gravel roadway circling his place just deep enough to bury a 30-gallon galvanized garbage can. Then loading the cans with bottles of booze, he lightly spread enough gravel over the closed top to hide the contents from view. When a customer arrived, Hydrick's man went out and brushed off the gravel, retrieving a bottle of hooch. Flowood Mayor Gary Rhoads said he backs the sale-by-the drink measure "not because I'm pro-liquor," emphasizing his goal is economic development. "I've heard from a number of substantial citizens urging legislation that would attract better restaurants and hotels to locate in our town." Chartered in 1953 on a mere dollop of land where a glass factory was located, Flowood, after several expansions, has grown to a City of 7,000. Now it surrounds the state's only international airport, Jackson's Thompson Field, and encompasses much of the rapidly developing business area along Lakeland Drive going east from Jackson. Rhoads and town leaders visualize several upscale restaurants and hotels locating near the airport and Lakeland Drive if they can offer wine and other libations in their dining facilities. Already, he says, "one or two of Jackson's better restaurants have indicated they would come if this bill passes and we vote for it." Flowood's legalization move would go nowhere unless 20 per cent of eligible voters petitioned for a referendum. A majority vote would then be required. Significantly, when Rankin County last rejected countywide legal liquor in 1995, Flowood voted in favor of legalization.

Soggy Sweat's Whiskey Speech

Noah S. "Soggy" Sweat Jr. served in the Mississippi state legislature from 1948 to 1952. He was twenty-four years old when he was elected. In later years, Sweat served as Alcorn County's district attorney during the State Line Gang days, was a circuit judge and was a college professor. The background and text of his rather infamous "Whiskey Speech" appears below. Sweat was still a young Mississippi legislator when he made this speech during a banquet at the King Edward Hotel in Jackson, Mississippi, in 1952. The debate about ending prohibition in Mississippi, one that would go on for another fourteen years, was a topic everywhere, including the banquet. Although Sweat's remarks are serious, he addressed both sides of the liquor issue with a combination of insight and a wicked sense of humor.

My friends, I had not intended to discuss this controversial subject at this particular time. However, I want you to know that I do not shun controversy. On the contrary, I will take a stand on any issue at any time, regardless of how fraught with controversy it might be. You have asked me how I feel about whiskey. All right, here is how I feel about whiskey. If when you say "whiskey" you mean the devil's brew, the poison scourge, the bloody monster, that defiles innocence, dethrones reason, destroys the home, creates misery and poverty, yea, literally takes the bread from the mouths of little children; if you mean the evil drink that topples the Christian man and woman from the pinnacle of righteous, gracious living into the bottomless pit of degradation and despair and shame and helplessness and hopelessness, then certainly I am against it. But if when you say "whiskey" you mean the oil of conversation, the philosophic wine, the ale that is consumed when good fellows get together, that puts a song in their hearts and laughter on their lips, and the warm glow of contentment in their eyes; if you mean Christmas cheer; if you mean the stimulating drink that puts the spring in the old gentleman's step on a frosty, crispy morning; if you mean the drink which enables a man to magnify his joy, and his happiness, and to forget, if only for a little while, life's great tragedies, and heartaches, and sorrows; if you mean that drink, the sale of which pours into our treasuries untold millions of dollars, which are used to provide tender care for our little crippled children, our blind, our deaf, our dumb, our pitiful aged and infirm, to build highways and hospitals and schools, then certainly I am for it. This is my stand. I will not retreat from it. I will not compromise.

A Disturbing Suspicion

By Hodding Carter, Editor and Publisher

Published on February 26, 1966
Delta Democrat-Times

There is gnawing suspicion in the mind of the man on the street that even with all the hoopla and strong talk coming out of the state capitol, nothing is going to be done about Mississippi's liquor posture. He is suspicious because of his knowledge of the past conduct of many members of our state legislature and the smoke screen which is thrown up to hide the issues each time the liquor question makes its way to the solemn chambers of the Senate and House of Representatives. He says he is tired of our hypocritical position when juries refuse to convict persons charged with possession of intoxicants or when they're charged with drunken driving, when the state levies taxes on contraband which is specifically illegal, when he has to duck and hide and wink at the law when he takes a drink.

YEAH, he say, yeah they do. A lot of talking down in Jackson, but in the end, they ain't gonna do a thing.

The bootleggers are going to get richer, and the crooked sheriffs and politicians and church folks are gonna still be happy because we got a dry law, because it's against the law in Mississippi to take a drink.

The man in the street has got a right to be suspicious.

On Thursday, the Senate finally passed Governor Johnson's bill, but it was a tattered version of its original form. And before it is submitted to the Governor for final action—if ever—it has to run the gauntlet of House action.

The most severely crippling amendment was the removal of highway patrol as an enforcement arm to stop the flow of whiskey into the state should it be voted dry in the projected April referendum.

Substituted in the patrol's place would be the National Guard, a unit we fully support in its orthodox function.

In all due respect to the guard, it is not, never has been, and never will be, a police organization; it is a military reserve force; trained for military and nothing else. It has no civil function.

In the past, the guard has been used by a succession of governors to make forays into Natchez and the Gulf Coast, Rankin County, and the Meridian area, but never has this organization been used for a sustained enforcement campaign.

It does not make good sense to us that the highway patrol, a superbly trained and equipped mobile force, can chase down murderers, bank robbers, safebreakers, auto and cattle thieves, speeders and drunken and reckless drivers, motorists who run red lights and stop signs, is prohibited by our lawmakers from exercising its powers against liquor law violators.

Does the legislature intend to let the enforcement problem return to rest on our sheriffs? The ridiculous record of most of these chief county law officers is answer enough.

More absurd is the amendment making it a felony to possess whiskey. Conviction for committing a felony means the culprit goes to Parchman for an indefinite period of time.

Coupled with the felony provision is another which demands harsher penalties for any law officer found guilty of not enforcing the prohibition law.

It is absolutely unreasonable to think that a jury of twelve good men and true would vote to send a man to Parchman for possession of whiskey when they rarely do so under the present statute which provides only a fine.

Just a few months ago a Hinds County Court could not find a dozen men to serve on a jury; they flatly advised the court they could not convict in a whiskey case even if the state proved beyond a reasonable doubt that the defendant was guilty.

As for the harsher penalties for officers—how many have been impeached or recalled under existing laws?

Until the legislators forget pressure from home counties, sectionalism, their own individual whims and fancies, and strive for an honest, intelligent, workable solution to our dilemma, we are inclined to agree with the man in the street.

Bibliography

Ancestry.com. "U.S. City Directories, 1821–1989" [database online].

Bailey, Reverend Thomas Jefferson. *Prohibition in Mississippi, Or Anti-Liquor Legislation from Territorial Days, with Its Results in the Counties.* Jackson, MS: Hederman Bros., 1907.

Barnwell, Marion, ed. *A Place Called Mississippi.* Jackson: University Press of Mississippi, 1997.

Barr, Dexter, Woodley Carter and Kenneth Stewart. "First Annual Report of the Alcoholic Beverage Control Division of the State Tax Commission to Gov. Paul B. Johnson." December 28, 1967.

Bayless, Luster. Telephone interview with the author, Ruleville, MS.

Bellande, Ray L. Biloxi Historical Society website. biloxihistoricalsociety.org. (Accessed June 6, 2014–July 31, 2014.)

Berman, Matt. *National Journal*, July 3, 2013.

Blackwell, Fred. Telephone interview with the author, Ridgeland, MS.

Bologna Brothers v. Morrissey, 154 So. 2d 455 (La. Ct. App. 1963). www.courtlistener.com/lactapp/9Q4u/bologna-brothers-v-morrissey. (Accessed June 6, 2014.)

Bolton, Charles C. *William F. Winter and the New Mississippi: A Biography.* Jackson: University of Mississippi Press, 2013.

———. "William F. Winter and the Politics of Racial Moderation in Mississippi." *Journal of Mississippi History* (n.d.).

Boudreaux, Edmond. *Legends and Lore of the Mississippi Golden Gulf Coast.* Charleston, SC: The History Press, 2013.

Bradshaw, Willie Mae. *Big Red*. Digital copy provided by Ken Hydrick Flessas. N.p.: Vantage Press, 1977.

Branch, James H. Telephone interview with the author, Birmingham, AL.

Branch, James L. Personal interview with the author, Ridgeland, MS.

Branch, Jim. Telephone interview with the author, Jackson, MS.

Burns, Ken, and Lynn Novick. *Prohibition*. Florentine Films and WETA, Public Broadcasting Service, 2011.

Caraway, Bill. *I Was There: An Autobiography*. N.p.: self-published, 1996.

Carter, Hodding. "The Bootlegger and Legalization." *Delta Democrat-Times*, July 25, 1952.

Cheeseborough, Steve. *Blues Traveling: The Holy Sites of Delta Blues*. Jackson: University Press of Mississippi, 2009.

Cobb, James. *The Most Southern Place on Earth*. Reprint, Oxford, UK: Oxford University Press, 1994.

Colby, Frank Moore, and Allen Leon Churchill. *New International Yearbook: A Compendium of the World's Progress*. New York: Dodd, Mead, and Company, 1914.

Cooper Postcard Collection. Mississippi Department of Archives and History. www.mdah.state.ms.us. (Accessed July 25, 2014.)

Coshocton (OH) *Tribune*. "Quotes from the News." May 15, 1966.

Davis, Brenda, curator, Mississippi State Capitol Building. Telephone interview with the author, Jackson, MS.

Dickerson, James. *Dixie's Dirty Little Secret*. Armonk, NY: M.E. Sharpe, Inc., 1998.

Dodgen, Kathy, administrative offices of Grand Gulf Military Park. Telephone interview with the author, Port Gibson, MS.

Echols, Donna. "'Black Market' Illegal Liquor Tax Was Hidden Away at Capitol." *Clarion-Ledger*, July 23, 2014.

———. E-mail correspondence with the author, August 14, 2014.

Farmers Service Administration, Digital Photograph Collection, Library of Congress. www.loc.gov. (Accessed May 10, 2014–July 31, 2014.)

Flessas, Ken. E-mail correspondence with the author, September 22, 2014.

Foreman, Harold. "Startling Testimony in Probe in Biloxi." *Delta Democrat-Times*, October 22, 1951.

Genealogy Bank. www.genealogybank.com. (Accessed August 15, 2014–October 6, 2014.)

Givens, Thomas P., administrative law judge (retired), SSA. Telephone interview with the author, Oxford, MS, and e-mail communication with the author, July 23, 2014.

————. "Whiskey, Chickens, and Cherry Bombs." usadeepsouth.ms11.net/whiskey.html. (Accessed June 7, 2014.)

Goins, Craddock. "Hooch and Homicide in Mississippi." *American Mercury*, October 1939.

Grand Gulf Military Park. www.grandgulfpark.state.ms.us. (Accessed June 10, 2014.)

Hailman, John. *From Midnight to Guntown*. Jackson: University Press of Mississippi, 2013.

Hanna, Rusty, assistant executive director, Enforcement, ABC Commission. Telephone interview with the author, Gluckstadt, MS, and e-mail communications between July 22, 2014, and September 22, 2014.

Henderson, Leslie, Lazy Magnolia Brewing Company, Kiln, MS. E-mail communication with the author, August 3, 2014.

Hendrickson, Paul. *Sons of Mississippi*. New York: Alfred Knopf, 2003.

Hofmann, Regan. "A Bootlegger's Dictionary: The Lexicon of Prohibition." raiseaglass.smithsonianchannel.com/blog/a-bootleggers-dictionary-the-lexicon-of-prohibition. (Accessed October 22, 2014.)

Holder, Harold D., and Cheryl J. Cherpitel. "End of Prohibition: A Case Study of Mississippi." *Contemporary Drug Problems*, June 22, 1996.

Humes, Edward. *Mississippi Mud: Southern Justice and the Dixie Mafia*. New York: Gallery Books, 2010.

Iglehart, Ferdinand Cowle. *King Alcohol Dethroned*. N.p.: Christian Herald Bible House, 1917.

Irwin, Will. "American Saloon." *Collier's Magazine*, March 21, 1908.

Jones, Charles, Alonzo E. Wilson and Fred D.L. Squires. *Prohibition Year 1910*. Chicago: National Prohibition Press, Lincoln Temperance Press, 1910.

Jones, Joe D. "As I See It." *Mississippi Business Journal*, August 9, 2004.

Joyce, Jaime. *Moonshine: A Cultural History of America's Liquor*. Minneapolis: Zenith Press, 2014.

Kincaid, Barbara. Personal interview with the author, Durant, MS.

Lally, Kathy. "A Journey from Racism to Reason." *Clarion Ledger*, January 5, 1997.

Lewis, Daryl, local historian. Telephone interview with the author, Leland, MS, and e-mail communications between July 7, 2014, and October 8, 2014.

Lindsey, Davie Ricardo. Telephone interview with the author, Flowood, MS.

Liquor Tax Laws, United States Congress, House Committee on Ways and Means. February 3 and 5, 1906. Washington, D.C.: U.S. Government Printing Office, 1906. books.google.com/books. (Accessed May 25, 2014–August 30, 2014.)

McCain Library and Archives, University of Southern Mississippi. Digital Photo Collections. www.lib.usm.edu. (Accessed August 5–7, 2014.)

McCarty, David. *Jackson Obscura, East Jackson, Part 1*. www.jacksonobscura. wordpress.com (Accessed May 20, 2014.)

McGraw, Jake. "Of Baptists, Bootleggers, and Brewmasters: Mississippi's Entry into the Craft Beer Movement." Rethink Mississippi, November 1, 2013. www.rethinkms.org/2013/11/01/craft-beer. (Accessed June 7, 2014.)

Minor, Bill. "Black Market Tax Mirrors Prohibition." *Daily Journal*. djournal. com/opinion/bill-minor-black-market-tax-mirrors-prohibition/minor.

———. "Liquor Bill Revives Memory of Rankin Bottle." *Daily Journal*. djournal.com/news/hedbill-minor-new-liquor-bill-revives-memory-of-rankin-bootle. (Accessed May 15, 2014.)

———. Telephone interview with the author, Jackson, MS.

Mississippi ABC Commission. www.dor.ms.gov/abc. (Accessed May 15, 2014–October 2, 2014.)

Mississippi Blues Trail. www.msbluestrail.org/blues-trail-markers/gold-coast. (Accessed May 15, 2014.)

Mississippi Department of Archives and History, Digital Photo Collections. www.mdah.state.ms.us. (Accessed August 1, 2014–October 16, 2014.)

Morrissey v. Bologna, 240 Miss. 284 (1960). law.justia.com/cases/mississippi/ supreme-court/1960/41525-0.html. (Accessed June 6, 2014.)

Morris, Willie. *My Mississippi*. Jackson: University Press of Mississippi, 2000.

———. *North Toward Home*. Boston: Houghton Mifflin Company, 2000.

Morris, W.R. *The State Line Mob*. Nashville: Rutledge Hill Press, 1990.

Nash, Jere, and Andy Taggart. *Mississippi Politics: The Struggle for Power, 1976–2006*. Jackson: University Press of Mississippi, 2006.

Nelson, Michael, and John Lyman Mason. *How the South Joined the Gambling Nation: The Politics of State Policy Innovation*. Baton Rouge: Louisiana State University Press. 2007.

Nesbit, Ross. Telephone interview with the author, Satartia, MS.

Newport (RI) *Daily News*. "48 Year Drought Nears End; Mississippi Prohibition." July 1, 1966.

NewspaperArchives.com. (Accessed July 6, 2014–October 15, 2014.)

Nicholson, Chet. *Dream Room: Tales of the Dixie Mafia*. Gulfport: Mississippi Sound Publishing, LLC, 2009.

Nuwer, Deanne S. "Gambling in Mississippi: Its Early History." Mississippi HistoryNow. mshistorynow.mdah.state.ms.us/articles/80/gambling-in-mississippi-its-early-history. (Accessed June 1, 2014.)

O'Brien, M.J. *We Shall Not Be Moved: The Jackson Woolworth's Sit-In and the Movement It Inspired.* Jackson: University Press of Mississippi, 2013.

Okrent, Daniel. *Last Call: The Rise and Fall of Prohibition.* New York: Scribner, 2010.

Owens, Elaine, director, Image and Sound, Mississippi Department of Archives and History. Telephone interview with the author, Jackson, MS, August 4, 2014.

Parchman State Penitentiary (Parchman Farm), Archive Department staff members. Interview with the author on May 22, 2014, and August 5, 2014.

Patrick, Richard, co-owner, Cathead Vodka. Telephone interview with the author, Gluckstadt, MS.

Peacock, Allen. Telephone interview with the author, Plano, TX, and e-mail correspondence with the author, June 9, 2014–July 10, 2014.

Powell, Gene Harlan. E-mail correspondence with the author, October 6, 2014, and October 22, 2014.

Rhodes, Andrew, special collection specialist, McCain Library and Archive, University of Southern Mississippi. Telephone interview with the author, August 5, 2014.

Risen, Clay. "How America Learned to Love Whiskey." *National Journal Magazine*, December 6, 2013.

Ritter, Norman. "A Tax on Lawbreakers Only." *Life* magazine, May 11, 1962. books.google.com/books. (Accessed September 18, 2014.)

Roberts, Keith. Telephone interview with the author, Tupelo, MS.

Robinson, Michelle, event coordinator and media director, Lazy Magnolia Brewing Company, Kiln, MS. E-mail communication with the author, August 4, 2014.

Smith, Hazel Brannon. "Looking at the Old South Through Hazel Eyes." aliciapatterson.org/stories/looking-old-south-through-hazel-eyes. (Accessed May 14, 2014.)

Spivak, Mark. *Moonshine Nation: The Art of Creating Cornbread in a Bottle.* Guilford, CT: Globe Pequot Press, 2014.

Stein, Bernard L. "This Female Crusading Scalawag, Hazel Brannon Smith, Justice, and Mississippi." www.freedomforum.org/publications/msj/courage.summer2000/y09.html. (Accessed May 15, 2014.)

Stentiford, Barry M. *The American Home Guard: The State Militia in the Twentieth Century.* College Station: Texas A&M University Press, 2002.

Stevens, Jerry. Telephone interview with the author, Jackson, MS.

Sullivan, Dr. William. "Perry Martin, Mississippi Bootlegger." *Delta Scene* magazine, Spring 1983.

Sumners, Cecil L. *The Governors of Mississippi*. Gretna, LA: Pelican Publishing, 1998.

Taylor, Cheryl, director, Museum of the Mississippi Delta. Personal interview with the author, Greenwood, MS, and e-mail communication, October 6, 2015.

Time magazine. "Liquor: Creeping Prohibition." November 15, 1943.

———. "Mississippi: Bourbon Borealis." February 11, 1966.

———. "The Press, the Last Word." November 21, 1955. content.time. com/time/magazine/article/0,9171,866658,00.html. (Accessed August 8, 2014.)

———. "Prohibition: Moonshine on the Rocks." November 4, 1966.

Trotter, B.J. Telephone interview with the author, Anderson, SC.

Turk, Dorothy. "Leland Mississippi from Hell-Hole to Beauty Spot." Leland Historical Foundation, 1986.

United States Brewers' Association, Yearbook, New York, 1916.

United States Senate. "Kefauver Crime Committee Launched." www.senate. gov/artandhistory/history/minute/Kefauver_Crime_Committee_ Launched.htm. (Accessed May 22, 2014.)

———. www.senate.gov. (Accessed July 8, 2014.)

Vanderleest, Anne, genealogy librarian, Brandon Public Library. Telephone interview with the author, Brandon, MS, and e-mail communications with the author between June 8, 2014, and October 9, 2014.

Walker, Pete. Telephone interview with the author, Ruleville, MS.

Weems, Charles H. *Agents That Fly: A Breed Apart II*. N.p.: SSI Publications, 1994.

Weems, Charles H., and W. Horace Carter. *A Breed Apart: A True Story About U.S. Treasury Agents During the Moonshine Years*. N.p.: SSI Publications, 1992.

Whalen, John A. *Maverick Among the Magnolias*. N.p.: Xlibris Corp., 2001.

Whitfield, A.H., T.C. Catchings and W.H. Hardy. *The Mississippi Code of 1906, of the Public Statute Laws, of the State of Mississippi*. N.p.: Brandon Printing Company, 1906.

Winkle, John W. *The Mississippi State Constitution: Oxford Commentaries on the State Constitutions of the United States*. Oxford, UK: Oxford University Press, 2011.

Woodward, Comer Vann. *Origins of the New South, 1877–1913*. Baton Rouge: Louisiana State University Press, 1971.

Yandle, Bruce. "Bootleggers, Baptists, and Bailed Out Bankers." The Freeman. www.fee.org/the_freeman/detail/bootleggers-baptists-and-bailed-out-bankers. (Accessed July 1, 2014.)

Yglesias, Matthew. "Ending Prohibition in Mississippi." September 30, 2010. thinkprogress.org/yglesias/2010/09/30/198686/ending-prohibition-in-mississippi. (Accessed May 20, 2014.)

Index

About the Author

J anice Branch Tracy is a sixth-generation Mississippian whose southern roots run deep in Attala and Holmes Counties. Born in the Mississippi Delta, she was raised in Jackson, Mississippi, where she graduated from Central High School. After attending the University of Mississippi, the author lived in several states while she pursued a thirty-year career with the U.S. government. After retiring in Dallas, Texas, the author started a blog entitled Mississippi Memories and was named one of the Top 40 Genealogy Blogs by *Family Tree Magazine* in 2011 and again in 2013. Her first book, *The Juke Joint King of the Mississippi Hills: The Raucous Reign of Tillman Branch*, was published by The History Press in March 2014. She is the mother of five children, stepmother to two daughters and grandmother of eleven grandchildren. In her spare time, she enjoys reading, gardening and occasional trips to explore new places. Presently, the author lives in North Texas with her husband, an adult son and a very fat tuxedo cat named Felix.